Boris Dänzer-Kantof

FULL STEAM AHEAD

A Golden Age
of Cruises

SCRIPTUM
EDITIONS

Page 1
Although cruising has become far more accessible over the last twenty years, the cruise lines still offer voyages inspired by the luxury cruises of earlier years. The service on board the ships of Regent Seven Seas Cruises, one of the more exclusive cruise lines now in operation, is as attentive as in any grand hotel.

Pages 2–3
The MSC cruise ship *MSC Poesia* (93,300 tonnes) in the Bay of Naples in the summer of 2008, on one of her first cruises. Her port of registry at that time was Venice.

Page 4
After leaving the shipyard of STX Europe Chantiers de l'Atlantique in December 2003, the *Queen Mary 2*, shown here at her moorings in the Brooklyn Cruise Terminal in New York, followed the *Queen Elizabeth 2* in providing the last great transatlantic crossing between Europe and North America from April to December every year. Since 2007, she has sailed every winter on exceptional world cruises.

Page 5
An officer of the Red Star Line on the bridge of the *Belgenland*, chartered by American Express for its first world cruise, a voyage of 133 days, from 4 December 1924 to 16 April 1925, with 384 passengers and no fewer than 600 crew.

Opposite
A 1930s album photograph shows passengers on a P&O Mediterranean cruise waiting for the tender that will take them back to their ship after an excursion.

Above right
A poster of 1926–7 advertising 'Holidays at Sea' in the Mediterranean and Africa, offered by a consortium of German companies.

Contents

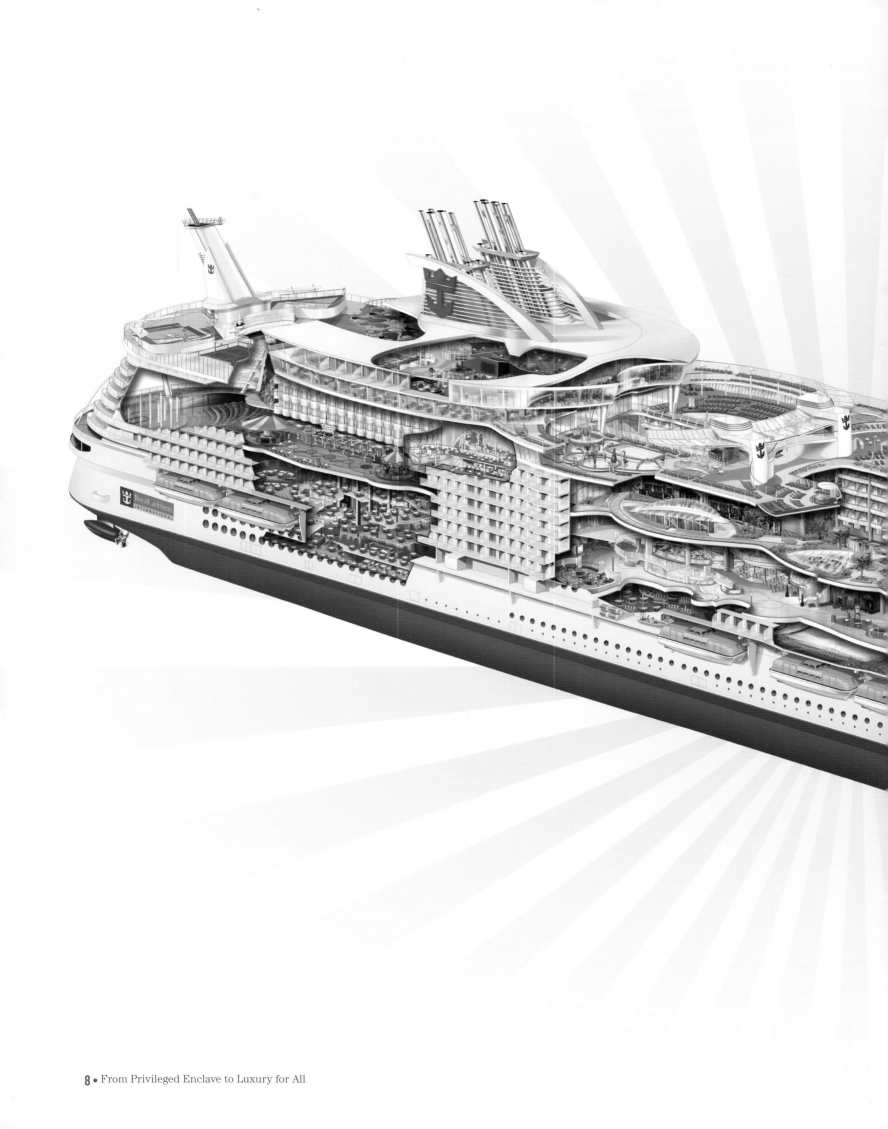

P&O TOURIST CLASS

United Fruit Company
luggage label, from a
Caribbean cruise on the
Peten in August 1936.

From Privileged Enclave to Luxury for All

Whether their destination is the North Cape or Sicily, South Africa or the Antarctic; whether they have Mexico, Martinique or Hawaii among their ports of call; whether they are a three-day excursion from Fort Lauderdale to Nassau, a month-long navigation of the Pacific, or a three-month voyage around the world; whether the boat is a luxury yacht of seventy cabins, a travel-worn cargo vessel with a hundred passenger berths, or a floating colossus of sixteen decks and four swimming pools, with over six thousand passengers in thirty-seven different categories of accommodation, cruising today is a multifarious world that has virtually nothing in common with cruises of the past. Except, of course, that it remains a world of superlatives. Yet it was from the humblest of beginnings that this leisure activity – which with each passing year is enticing enthusiasts in ever-growing numbers, especially in Europe – began in the late nineteenth century.

As rail and sea transport developed from the 1840s, railway and steamer companies played a major part in the democratization of travel as a leisure activity. In the wake of the pleasure excursions offered by the railway companies at all-inclusive prices, European ship-owners, whose fleets were largely engaged in transporting freight, mail, immigrants and passengers travelling for work or family reasons, began to organize pleasure trips at sea. In many languages, the word 'cruise' (*croisière, Kreuzfahrt, crociere, crucero*, and so on) did not

even exist in this context until after 1900; before that time it was used to describe the actions of cruisers, warships that patrolled the seas and intercepted enemy shipping. These pleasure excursions –remarkable early precursors of the modern cruise – were one-off events, organized for a specific purpose according to a pre-arranged itinerary including scenic ports of call, and invariably reserved for a tiny number of privileged passengers.

The Question of Origins

One of the first of these organized excursions – still claimed by P&O (the Peninsular and Oriental Steam Navigation Company) as the very first leisure cruise – took place in 1844, when the *Iberia* toured the Mediterranean, calling in at Vigo, Porto, Lisbon, Cadiz, Gibraltar, Malta, Athens, Smyrna Constantinople and Alexandria, with an excursion to Cairo. On board were some forty passengers, including – at the company's invitation – the writer William Makepeace Thackeray. In his *Notes of a Journey from Cornhill to Cairo*, 'performed in the steamers of the Peninsular and Oriental Company', published two years later (under the *nom de plume* M.A. Titmarsh), Thackeray urged all those with sufficient time and funds at their disposal to venture to share his experience. As several steamers had been pressed into service – the *Lady Mary Wood* and the *Tagus* as well as the *Iberia* – to complete this tour, it cannot strictly speaking be described as a cruise, however. Another early sea voyage that had all the appearance of a cruise, but wasn't quite, was the 'Great Pleasure Excursion' undertaken by Mark Twain from New York to the Holy Land on board the *Quaker City* in 1867. This first organized intercontinental sea trip for tourists was to form the main inspiration of *The Innocents Abroad*, published in 1869.

The advertisement that Robert Miles Sloman placed in the *Leipziger Illustrierte Zeitung* in January 1845 may be considered, by contrast, as a blueprint for the late-nineteenth-century cruise. As Bernhard Huldermann relates, the Anglo-German Hamburg-based ship owner was offering a world cruise the following summer on one of his steamers: 'All the ship's amenities and accommodation, the time spent in the various ports of call, and every last detail of the excursion were calculated with the sole aim of promoting the safety, comfort, entertainment and education of the passengers. Admission on board would be strictly reserved for persons of spotless reputation and good education, and preference would be given to those of a scientific persuasion. The members of the expedition could be quite confident of enjoying of a successful and enjoyable voyage. A first-class vessel, a cultivated and experienced captain, a specially selected crew and a qualified doctor were guaranteed to complete the success of the enterprise. The price of such a voyage was so low as to represent only a modest supplement to the normal cost of life on land. In return, the passenger would enjoy numerous opportunities to acquire a first-hand experience of the wonders of the world, to gaze on the glorious landscapes of the most untamed lands, and to glimpse the customs and traditions of many different countries. During the voyage, he would be surrounded by the greatest comforts and would enjoy the company of his refined and cultivated fellow-passengers. The sea air would bring incalculable benefits for his health, and the experience would remain a pleasure for him to draw on for the rest of his lifetime.' The 'health' argument was to be revisited in the 1880s by medical men who, in the *British Medical Journal*, praised such sea voyages for their curative virtues.

Left
In 1894, the transatlantic liner *La Touraine* – launched in 1891, when it was the largest French liner by tonnage, and the fifth largest in the world – made the first cruise organized by the French Line, to the Mediterranean from New York. Cover of a brochure intended for the American market, proposing a cruise to the Mediterranean, the Orient and the Holy Land in 1896.

So what is a cruise; how can it be defined? For the maritime historian Arnold Kludas, it is a vacation that may last anything from a few days to several months, on a specially equipped boat, with pre-arranged ports of call chosen for their beauty or interest, and adequate time allowed for excursions, whether individual or organized. The operator who plans and arranges it should advertise it on a regular basis, producing brochures containing all relevant details sufficiently in advance, so that potential passengers can make their reservations. The ships should engage in no other commercial activity for the duration of the cruise. Once on board, the passengers should be not only safe but also comfortable, with all the amenities of a hotel, including accommodation, restaurants and entertainment. According to this definition, narrow though it may be, it was in the 1880s that cruising really took off. According to Kludas, the first cruise was made in 1877 by the steam coaster *Wanaka* of the British Union Steam Ship Company of New Zealand, and remained within coastal waters. The first vessel to be dedicated specifically to cruises was John Clark's *Ceylon*, which from 1858 had been a P&O steamer before being converted into a cruise ship in 1881 – so enabling P&O to claim the invention of the cruise a second time. The first ship to be designed for the sole purpose of pleasure cruising was the *St Sunniva* of the North of Scotland, Orkney & Shetland Steam Navigation Company. This yacht-like vessel was built in 1887, but from 1908 was converted into a ferry. In 1889, the Orient Steam Navigation Company adapted two of its steamers on the London–Australia route, *Chimborazo* and *Garonne*, in order to cruise the ports of the Baltic and Norway, as well as the Mediterranean. Between that year and 1900, this company was to offer an annual timetable of 'pleasure cruises', numbering ninety-five in all.

Although the Compagnie Générale Transatlantique carried out its first cruise on 19 August 1883, when the three-masted steamer *Pereire* sailed from Pauillac for Biarritz and A Coruña with the company's founders, Isaac and Emile Pereire, on board, it was not until 1894 that it offered a selection of regular cruises aboard *La Touraine*, *Le Général Chanzy* and *La Gascogne*.

Albert Ballin, Inventor of the Modern Cruise

The earliest 'pleasure cruises' were often pleasurable only in name: so rudimentary were the amenities on board and in the ports of call that voyages remained an ordeal. Now more than ever before on transatlantic steamers, the ambition of ship owners – and primarily of Albert Ballin, the young director of the German Hamburg–Amerikanische Packetfahrt-Actien-Gesellschaft (Hapag), also known as the Hamburg–America Line – was to free their passengers from all the constraints that had hitherto been considered as an unavoidable feature of sea travel, and to guarantee them all the comforts of a luxury hotel. These included spacious cabins with comfortable beds (bunk beds were gradually banished); an effective ventilation system; electricity and en suite bathrooms; elegantly decorated and spacious public rooms, often lit by glazed roofs and dedicated to different activities (entrance foyer with lift, dining room or restaurant, drawing room, music room, library or reading room, smoking room, ladies' room, mechanotherapy room, and so on); a promenade deck with a substantial awning to provide shelter from the sun and fumes; kitchens and catering worthy of the finest restaurants; armies of highly attentive staff; interesting ports of call; and pre-planned excursions.

On 22 January 1891, 240 passengers (an unprecedented number on a voyage of this kind), including Albert Ballin and

Left
Brochure for a Norwegian
cruise on the *Blücher* of
the Hapag line.

Opposite
This photograph from
a private album shows
passengers gathered for
a souvenir picture on the
accommodation ladder of
the Hapag ship *Meteor*,
during a Norwegian cruise
departing from Hamburg,
form 6 to 14 June 1913.

Overleaf
One of the 120 cabins on
board the Hapag line's
Prinzessin Victoria Luise,
named in June 1900 and
the first vessel designed
as a cruise ship.

his wife, sailed from the port of Cuxhaven on board the express steamer *Augusta Victoria* for a fifty-seven-day Mediterranean cruise. 'Ensure the comfort of our compatriots on the high seas,' Kaiser Wilhelm II – who was himself fond of sea voyages – declared to them, 'and it will be to the benefit of both your company and the Nation as a whole.' Considered as the first modern cruise, this voyage – which included a dozen ports of call and numerous excursions on land – had been planned in detail a year in advance, in cooperation with international tourist agencies and in spite of the scepticism of most of the company management. For Albert Ballin, its fiery young director, the 'pleasure cruise' was not so much a new form of leisure activity as a solution to an economic problem: as far as he was concerned it was chiefly a way of making the fleet profitable during the winter season, when bookings for the transatlantic crossing were virtually wiped out by the bad weather conditions in the North Atlantic, forcing the steamers to lie idle in their home ports. Laying them up for the winter was costly, and cruising could avoid it.

The success of this tourist cruise (with passengers of ten different nationalities on board), repeated the following year from New York, and every year thereafter except during the Great War, encouraged other companies to offer similar services. For John Burns, president of Hapag's rival Cunard, there could be no doubting the merits of Ballin's initiative. On the fiftieth anniversary of Hapag, celebrated on the *Augusta Victoria*, he wrote to him: 'Your company ... has truly fulfilled expectations in offering accommodation of the highest luxury and comfort for visiting places of interest, both ancient and modern, throughout the world, and in rendering such peregrinations, hitherto the source of anxiety and difficulties, as easy to undertake as a daily journey on the railway.'

As increasing numbers of people started to travel at the end of the nineteenth century, the cruise began to appear as a new and exclusive preserve for the elite of society, where the upper classes could hobnob with each other. Mediterranean cruises were swiftly followed by voyages to Norway and the Arctic, made popular by Kaiser Wilhelm II, then from 1896 to the Caribbean, and finally around the world. While luxury trains and international hotels were expanding, Albert Ballin – who had stayed in many of the finest hotels, especially in Paris and London – built the first two ocean liners designed exclusively for cruises, the *Prinzessin Victoria Luise* and the more modest *Meteor*, both fitted out like luxury yachts. Gradually, the status of ships changed: no longer merely a form of transport, they now became an integral part of the cruise. As Dr William T. Corlett of Cleveland observed after a Caribbean cruise in 1908 aboard the liner *Oceana*, bought by Hapag from the Union Castle Line in order to become a dedicated cruise ship, 'It's strange how quickly one feels at home on a ship.'

Once on board, one of the areas of highest expectation surrounded the pleasures of the table. And as on transatlantic liners, it was mealtimes, proclaimed at fixed times by a bugle call, that punctuated the day. By 1929, when Evelyn Waugh went on a Mediterranean cruise aboard the *Stella Polaris*, little had changed: 'On the *Stella* everybody seemed to eat all the time. They had barely finished breakfast – which included on its menu, besides all the dishes usually associated with that meal, such solid fare as goulash and steak and onions – before tureens of clear soup appeared. Luncheon was at one o'clock and was chiefly remarkable for the cold buffet which was laden with every kind of Scandinavian delicatessen, smoked salmon, smoked eels,

venison, liver pies, cold game and meat and fish, sausage, various sorts of salad, eggs in sauces, cold asparagus, in almost disconcerting profusion. At four there was tea, at seven a long dinner, and at ten dishes of sandwiches, not of the English railway-station kind, but little rounds of bread covered with caviar and *foie gras* with eggs and anchovies.'

Here too, Albert Ballin's foresight was to gain the advantage for German cruise liners: he introduced the first 'Ritz-Carlton Restaurant' à la carte menu on board the *Kaiserin Auguste Victoria*, a year after inaugurating it on the transatlantic liner *Amerika*, thanks to the involvement of the great chef Auguste Escoffier. Gastronomic indulgence and excursions aside, leisure activities on board were few. It was up to cruise passengers to fill the idle hours in their own way: loafing in the sun, chatting with other passengers, reading, organizing private parties, joining photography clubs, going to balls (masked or otherwise), or exercising in a small room set aside for the purpose, often on the sun deck. Gradually the shipping companies offered organized activities to fill up the leisure time between ports of call, with games and social activities including deck games such as shuffleboard, wooden horse races, bingo and tennis matches. At the same time, a greater variety of services was also provided, such as a nursery, laundry, hairdressing salon, photographer's studio and shops.

Despite the growing numbers of ships now reserved for pleasure, cruising remained of secondary importance on the high seas. The First World War dealt it a severe blow, from which it would take a number of years to recover. After the war, most of the German cruise fleet was seized by the Allies: the Cunard White Star Line received the majority of its vessels, including the *Imperator*, renamed the *Berengaria*, while Canadian Pacific

acquired the *Kaiserin Auguste Victoria*, which became the *Empress of Scotland*, and the *Tirpitz*, renamed the *Empress of Australia*. These liners were to become the lynchpin of the commercial transatlantic fleet of the 1920s.

The 'Booze Cruise' to the Rescue

The reduction of American immigration quotas in 1923, followed by the Wall Street crash of 1929, led to a massive falling off in the numbers of steerage passengers, who had hitherto provided a regular and profitable source of income for the transatlantic lines. Feeling the ill effects of this, European shipping companies set about finding replacement markets. Unwittingly, the American government was to lend impetus to cruises from the 1920s. The Prohibition laws, introduced in 1919, forbade the consumption of alcohol on American soil – which meant that shipping companies could offer a new type of vacation. These 'cruises to nowhere' spent a weekend, three or four days, or even a week out in the middle of the Atlantic, often without any ports of call, for the sole purpose of enabling passengers to indulge in the ship's 'facilities'. No sooner had the vessel reached the three-mile limit and entered international waters than the champagne corks started popping and the alcohol flowing, with complete impunity. For the first time, as Daniel Okrent has argued, the ships themselves became the destination of the cruise.

Veritable life-savers for wealthy drinkers, these 'booze cruises' were to lend a fresh impetus to the pleasure cruise, even after Prohibition ended in 1933. This was a niche market that the shipping lines were only too happy to service, deploying legendary if elderly liners such as Cunard's *Berengaria* and *Aquitania*, the White Star Line's *Olympic*, *Britannic* and *Majestic*, and

even the United States Line's *George Washington*, though without ever stating the true purpose of these trips in their brochures. The famous *Belgenland*, flagship of the Red Star Line, invented the idea of 'showboat cruises', six-day events devoted exclusively (officially) to vaudeville acts including – under the supervision of William Morris, impresario of Charlie Chaplin and the Marx Brothers – magic shows and gymnastics, revues and singing acts. But as the brochure for the summer of 1931 made clear, there were other attractions too: 'her cellars will be filled with a selection of the finest drinks from Europe'. Passengers on the *Belgenland* would sip these on the lido deck, relaxing around the swimming pools with tons of sand from the beaches of Ostend to run between their toes. The *Leviathan*, meanwhile, which for a long time had suffered from being a 'dry' ship as it sailed under the American flag, was finally granted permission to serve alcohol outside American waters in the 1920s, and promptly installed its own on-board brewery. So great were the quantities of alcohol consumed that passengers renamed the smoking room the 'drinking room'.

The lure of alcohol was so irresistible that the shipping companies installed extra bars on their liners, and trained their crews in how to deal with their parched American passengers. On non-English-speaking vessels, cabin crew and deck boys learned enough English to direct passengers to the bars; the bar staff, meanwhile, pored over the names and recipes of the Americans' favourite cocktails – the Bronx, Dry Martini, Manhattan and Old Fashioned – and took care not to muddle their maraschino cherry, olive, lemon slice and orange zest garnishes. In 1924, a French Line brochure, quoted by John Maxtone-Graham, promised: 'As you head out to sea, out of reach of amendments and prohibitions of all kinds, those dear little iced confections start to

appear, twinkling on their slender crystal stems ... so French, so innocent and so lip-smackingly delicious.' But this new clientele was not to everyone's taste. Like the passengers on traditional cruises and transatlantic crossings, Pierre Thoreux, captain of the original *France*, the 'floating palace' built in 1912, which in the early 1930s made some triangular cruises departing from and returning to New York via Halifax and Bermuda, was distinctly unimpressed by these new American passengers, who were attracted purely by the French wines and spirits on board, which they consumed in abundance once in the safety of international waters. In his memoirs he recalled: 'Some of them took no notice even of the ports of call, which in their eyes were very much of secondary interest. As they left the ship in New York, they talked nostalgically of the "good times" they had had on board.'

Antidote to the Depression

According to John Maxtone-Graham, self-confessed 'sea-addict' and veteran of hundreds of transatlantic crossings, cruises were quite simply 'the perfect antidote to post-Depression depression'. These modestly priced short cruises in the Atlantic or to more affordable destinations such as Nova Scotia in Canada, Bermuda or the Bahamas from the little Florida port of Miami – which was doing well out of the building boom and the proximity of Havana – represented only one section of the market for cruises at this period. The classic itineraries – longer and therefore costlier, and frequented by a clientele that remained largely drawn from the wealthy elite – also brought in a comfortable revenue during the off-season. Surprisingly, as the number of available berths rose so did the demand for them, despite the worldwide economic crisis. One reason for this was undoubtedly the deployment in the

Right
Designed for the warm waters of the Caribbean, the four sister ships of the Grace Line – *Santa Rosa*, *Santa Paula*, *Santa Elena* and *Santa Lucia* – boasted a dining room with a retractable roof so that passengers could dine under the stars. It was not unusual, however, for guests to ask for the roof to be closed again because of smuts from the ship's funnels.

Opposite
The *Augustus*, launched in 1927 by the Italian company NGI, a year after her sister ship *Roma*, was endowed with a small tiled sea water swimming pool positioned between her funnels, surrounded by sunbeds and parasols to create the illusion of being on the Lido in Venice.

1920s and 30s of a new fleet which, though not dedicated exclusively to cruising, was modern and more luxurious.

Major improvements in the design and facilities of this new generation of ocean liners were to play a decisive part in making cruises more comfortable. Now public rooms and even cabins were air-conditioned; most cabins had en suite bathrooms and some had private balconies; dining rooms were equipped with retractable roofs; and there were outside swimming pools, fitness suites and spas. More and more transatlantic liners were designed with this dual function in mind: the Canadian Pacific's *Empress of Britain* was fitted out with a tennis court, for instance, and the Norwegian American Line's *Olosfjord* boasted high-level restaurants on the promenade deck – a first for this transatlantic liner that was dedicated largely to cruising. Italian liners, more open to the outside and with their decks covered with sand and parasols, meanwhile added a note of glamour to the world of the cruise.

Although the clientele was largely American, the operators remained dominated by European – and especially German – companies. Forced to start again from scratch after the First World War, the German lines offered spanking new boats that included some of the largest and most popular of all cruise liners, such as Norddeutscher Lloyd's *Columbus* and *Sierra Cordoba*, Hapag's *Reliance*, *Resolute* and *Milwaukee*, and Hamburg Süd's *Cap Polonio* and *Cap Arcona*. As for the American companies, with the exception of Matson in the South Pacific and the Alaska Steamship Company in Alaska, the majority of cruises on regular routes were offered by freight companies whose vessels plied the Caribbean or South American waters with cargos of bananas (the United Fruit Company), bauxite (the Alcoa Line)

or a range of goods (Moore-McCormack and the Grace Line), while also making several dozen cabins – usually extremely comfortable – available to cruise passengers. The Grace Line offered cruises on its new mixed-cargo Santa fleet – boasting retractable roofs so that passengers could dine under the stars, cosy public rooms, en suite bathrooms and a passenger capacity of over two hundred and fifty – that were to prove increasingly popular in the United States.

Celebrated cruise ships of this era include Bergen Line's elegant *Stella Polaris* and the Blue Star Line's *Arandora Star*. The first, with its air of an imperial yacht, had a crew of 130 to welcome 200 cosseted passengers. A day on the second, meanwhile, which had started her career as a refrigerated transporter for Argentinian beef, cost the equivalent of the average week's pay; between 1929 and 1939, the *Arandora Star* sailed on 124 cruises, one each in the Baltic and the Indian Ocean, six in the Caribbean, twelve to the Canaries, and the rest in the Mediterranean and the fjords of Norway. As for the *Normandie*, the quintessence of the Art Deco ocean liner and acme of 1930s' shipbuilding (she was the first to be equipped with radar, turbo-electric propulsion, and a comprehensive and efficient air-conditioning system), her hundred or so transatlantic crossings from 1935 paled in contemporary eyes in comparison with the only two cruises of her short career. These were to the West Indies in 1938 and 1939, both culminating at Rio de Janeiro, a tropical millionaires' club and a city of legendary status in the American imagination. The Compagnie Générale Transatlantique spent over a year making the preparations and choosing the ports of call for this cruise, as the considerable draught of the *Normandie* – the largest liner in the world to cross the Equator – meant that she could not drop anchor at

all the ports of the Caribbean. The logistics of keeping the ship supplied with provisions, oil and water also had to be addressed, and timetables and excursions worked out. The itinerary for 1938 sailed from New York to Nassau, Port of Spain, Rio de Janeiro, Fort-de-France and back to New York, all in twenty-five days. The 1939 cruise added a port of call at Bridgetown, Barbados.

No sooner had the advertisements appeared in the press than all the cabins on this single-class cruise – though cabins ranged from tourist class at $395 to suites at $8600 – were reserved by 975 of the super-rich (an unprecedented number of passengers on a cruise), with just two French passengers among an otherwise exclusively American clientele. Dubbed the 'million-dollar cruise', it took with it in the ship's holds and cold storage, it was said, 150,000 bottles of champagne ordered from Le Havre, a tonne of lobsters and two tonnes of Beluga caviar. The Boston-based Raymond-Whitcomb agency, commissioned to provide the entertainment, engaged New York artistes including magicians, singers, dancers and jugglers. Although it was initially turned down by the French Line, the latest Walt Disney cartoon, *Snow White and the Seven Dwarves*, had its première in the ship's cinema.

A week after sailing from the French Line's Quay 88, the French liner glided slowly into the magnificent Guanabara Bay, strewn with rocks and islands and overlooked by the famous Sugarloaf Mountain. The local newspapers were captivated by the sight of 'The world's biggest and most beautiful ship in the world's most beautiful harbour'. Every day, several thousand Brazilians presented themselves at the gangway, invitation in hand, for a tour of the *Normandie*. As most of these special permits were forgeries, these visits were cut short, to the immense disappointment – turning to anger – of the Brazilians who had bought them unknowingly and who had waited patiently for hours on the quayside. Happily this incident played out at the height of Carnival, and was soon forgotten. A grand dinner on board ship, in a dining room that was eleven metres longer than the Hall of Mirrors at Versailles, followed by a ball, brought this week-long stay in Rio by the flagship of the French Line to a close. Before setting sail for the Lesser Antilles, the liner executed a sort of 'sail-past' in tribute to the land that had given it such a welcome: 'I passed as close as possible to the shore so that our passengers could admire for one last time the wonderful panorama of this country whose population and press had given us such a warm reception,' explained Captain Pierre Thoreux.

It was in the Café-Grill on the second cruise, in 1939, that the reputation of Brazil's first international star was sealed. Noticed at the Casino da Urca, and invited to perform on board the *Normandie* with her band, Bando da Lua, Maria do Carmo Miranda signed her first American contract with the Broadway impresario Lee Shubert, so becoming Carmen Miranda, the 'Brazilian bombshell'.

There can be no disputing that the flagship of the Compagnie Générale Transatlantique offered the most sumptuous cruise in maritime history; it should also be remembered, however, that from now on the shipping companies set their sights on a new and more modest clientele for their magnificent cruise ships.

From Middle Class to Tourist Class: The New Clienteles

In order to attract the American middle classes, who were increasingly seduced by the idea of vacationing at sea, as well as the many students who were setting off to discover Europe, many shipping lines decided to convert their third-class accommodation into a new 'tourist class', and to offer a greater variety of tickets at modest prices as well as all-inclusive deals. While second class gradually disappeared, first class – now 'cabin class' – became more luxurious. Its accommodation remained in the same position, at the centre of the ship, between the promenade deck and the saloon deck, while the other classes were placed in the stern, less comfortable because of the vibrations of the propellers, or the prow. Not until the appearance of the Holland America Line's *Rotterdam* in 1959 was a horizontal division of the classes adopted. But this new system was to last only a decade: by the late 1960s the classes had disappeared – with the cruise ships themselves following suit soon after.

While the clientele remained 80 per cent American, new sections of the public interested in this type of leisure activity began to appear. According to the essayist John Malcolm Brinnin, 'At the start of its debut, the cruise ship was the exclusive preserve of the seriously rich and those who had, or pretended to, social eminence. Within the space of thirty years, the cruise ship would become an excursion boat available to almost anyone with ten days and a few hundred dollars to spare.' Although segregation by class was the rule on their regular routes, some companies offered only a single class on board their transatlantic liners, and their transpacific liners when crossing the southern seas out of season, as we have seen with the *Normandie* cruise in 1938. The

only distinction that remained was the choice of cabin. Elsewhere on the ship, all passengers – whether they were captains of industry, people of private means, shareholders, businessmen, government officials or employees – rubbed shoulders together on the promenade deck, in the swimming pool and in the dining room. To the annoyance of the select few, the public rooms, formerly so delightfully empty, were now filled to bursting, in what the historian Marie-Françoise Berneron-Couvenhes has called 'the transition from a luxury that was rare and elitist to a luxury that was vulgar and commonplace'. Evelyn Waugh, meanwhile, was characteristically caustic about 'those pitiable droves of Middle West school teachers whom one encounters suddenly at street corners and in public buildings, baffled, breathless, their heads singing with unfamiliar names, their bodies strained and bruised from scrambling in and out of motor charabancs, up and down staircases, and from trailing disconsolately through miles of gallery and museum at the heels of a facetious and contemptuous guide.'

It was the German lines who began the true democratization of cruising, with their introduction in the late 1920s of the 'package cruise'. The Monte class liners of the Hamburg Süd line, notably, designed from 1926 to carry European immigrants to South America rather then the United States, offered only two classes, third and steerage, and in summer were given over to reasonably priced cruises of the Norwegian fjords, the Mediterranean, and even the grandiose glaciers of Tierra del Fuego. Unlike Hapag and NDL, which offered an international clientele, largely American and English, luxury amenities including single-berth cabins, winter gardens, lavish salons lit by glass roofs, covered swimming pools, tennis courts and naturally-lit dining rooms with sea views, liners such as the *Monte*

Sarmiento and *Monte Olivia* offered German passengers of modest means simple but functional public rooms, cabins of two to eight berths (with married couples given priority for two-berth ones), and large dormitories for twelve to twenty-four passengers. 'We are particularly anxious to emphasize that on these voyages described as "popular",' a Hamburg Süd brochure quoted by the maritime historian Arnold Kludas was at pains to point out, 'every luxury that is usually found in the first-class accommodation of the cruise liners that generally serve the countries of the north has been avoided. The *Monte Sarmiento* is a third-class liner of the modern type. Passengers may move around the vessel in a relaxed manner wearing ordinary tourist dress. We therefore ask that you bring on board only the necessary clothing. A man, for example, may bring, in addition to the suit he is wearing, a spare suit and a reasonably heavy coat, if possible a rug for going on deck, a spare pair of boots and the usual underwear for sixteen days. Evening dress is not required.'

The shipping companies vied with each other in dreaming up ideas to attract a popular clientele. From 1927–8, Hamburg Süd introduced *billigen Reisen*, or 'reasonably priced trips', which notably included all trips in the ticket price. In 1931, Hapag brought in *Seefahrten*, or 'sea voyages' on board the *Reliance* and the *Resolute*, consisting of mini-cruises that left Hamburg at midday and ended at Cuxhaven two days later, after steaming along the Norwegian coast without making landfall. But without any ports of call, could these really be called cruises? By contrast, the Christmas and New Year cruise to the islands of the Atlantic, offered by the Hamburg company for the first time in December 1933, was so successful that it was immediately taken up by the NDL and Hamburg Süd, and was set to become a classic.

In spite of the Depression and the disastrous financial position of the German shipping lines, as soon as the Nazis came to power in 1933 they decided to keep the transatlantic routes and cruises going for the sake of their international standing. From 1934, the organization that now ruled over the leisure time of German workers, 'Kraft durch Freude' or KdF ('Strength Through Joy', a subsidiary organization of the Deutsche Arbeitsfront, or German Labour Front), took over cruising as an important propaganda tool for mass tourism, and for the encouragement abroad of an image that was altogether suaver and less antipathetic than that created by the SA and SS. 'Now we are all emperors,' trumpeted Nazi propaganda, in an allusion to the cruises initiated by Kaiser Wilhelm II. The KdF quickly became one of the largest tour operators in the world, chartering a good proportion of the German cruise ship fleet in order to send thousands of Germans to the North Sea and the Norwegian fjords, but also to the Mediterranean and especially to Italy (with ports of call including Naples, Palermo and Venice), in partnership with its Italian equivalent, the Opera Nazionale Dopolavoro (National Recreational Club); to the islands of the Atlantic (the Canaries and Balearics); and even to exotic Tripoli in Libya, then a colony of Fascist Italy.

The KdF even built its own cruise ships, such as the *Wilhelm Gustloff*, launched in May 1937, and the *Robert Ley*, an authentic prototype for the cruise ships of today, capable of accommodating 2000 people including crew, with no distinctions between classes, and with vast outside decks for morning flag ceremonies, exercises and communal games; an auditorium; two dance floors; a swimming pool; a gymnasium; and spacious cabins, all with portholes looking out to sea and hot and cold running

Cunard White Star   *The New CARONIA*

water. In the six years from 1934 to 1939, nearly 800,000 passengers set off on 673 seven-day cruises at very affordable prices – though at the added cost of being subjected to propaganda broadcast on board from loudspeakers, to discreet surveillance by the authorities, and to deprivation of any privacy. According to Harmut Berghoff, Nazi propaganda presented the KdF cruises as 'an upper-middle-class privilege made available to the general public', but in reality only one worker in a hundred was able to take advantage of these cruises, or less then 20 per cent of all those who went on Strength Through Joy cruises.

The Cruise Revival

Sea travel now became a 'deliberate choice aimed at pleasure', in the expression of Marie-Françoise Berneron-Couvenhes. But the Second World War was to put an abrupt end to travel for pleasure, which not surprisingly had disastrous consequences for the shipping lines. On the Allied side, many popular cruise ships such as the *Empress of Britain, Empress of Canada, Arandora Star, Carinthia* and *Laconia* were torpedoed and sunk by U-Boats in the battle that raged in the Atlantic. Other ships requisitioned for use as transporters for troops and equipment remained in military service until the late 1940s. The liners of the German fleet – including the legendary *Columbus, Cap Arcona, Resolute, Bremen, Wilhelm Gustloff, Robert Ley, Steuben, Monte Sarmiento, Monte Olivia, Monte Pascoal* and *Deutschland* –were either seized or destroyed at the end of conflict, meaning that the fleet had to be built up from scratch once more, never to regain its pre-war importance.

In both Europe and the United States, obsolete liners were converted into cruise ships, while new 'dual-purpose' liners with spacious cabins were launched from the shipyards; the most famous of these were the *Caronia* of 1947, *Kungsholm* and *Arcadia* (1953), *Carinthia* (1956), *Jean Mermoz* (1958), *Canberra* (1960), *France* (1961), *Raffaello* and *Michelangelo* (1965) and *Queen Elizabeth 2* (1969). For the shipping lines, cruise ships became once again an occasional means of minimizing losses out of season, with the notable exception of the Cunard Line's *Caronia*. Designed for a highly discerning clientele, this classically beautiful 34,000-tonne liner and cruise ship proved a success because her transatlantic crossings were aimed solely at positioning her in a new cruising area. Her itinerary was the same every year: sailing round the world, or making a detour round Africa during the early months of the year, in spring she embarked on cruises in the Mediterranean and Black Sea, before spending the summer in Scandinavia and the Atlantic and ending the year in the Caribbean. Very advanced for her time, the 'Green Goddess' (as she was nicknamed after her livery in four shades of pale green, designed to protect against the tropical heat) was also distinguished from traditional transatlantic liners by her terraced decks, permanent outside pool, running hot and cold water in private bathrooms, and constant renovations and updates of amenities. She also boasted one of the best ratios of crew to passengers, approaching one to one. Her 500 passengers felt so at home on board that some even made the ship their year-round home: the American Clara L. MacBeth spent nearly fifteen years living in the same cabin, at a cost of some $20 million.

The *Caronia* was an exception, however, as the majority of postwar liners remained ill-adapted to cruising: their internal arrangements did not allow a rapid transition from a configuration for several classes to just one, swimming pools were rare or

Getting there is half the *fun!*

AUTUMN is ideal for your visit to Europe . . . when Britain
and the Continent are at their sparkling, uncrowded best . . . and ideal, too,
for a gay, relaxing ocean voyage! When you go Cunard, each day at sea
and each brilliant, enchanted evening is a glorious new adventure shared with interesting companions
amid all the comforts of a great seaside resort. You'll delight in the bright conviviality, the thoughtful,
attentive service for which Cunard is famous . . . and the marvelous food,
prepared for your sea-sharpened appetite by internationally trained chefs.
See your travel agent about Cunard's lower "Thrift Season" rates.

Swimming Pool in the Queen Mary

No wonder more people prefer CUNARD

From New York: QUEEN ELIZABETH • QUEEN MARY • MAURETANIA • CARONIA • BRITANNIC • MEDIA • PARTHIA
From Canada: FRANCONIA • SCYTHIA • SAMARIA • ASCANIA

too small, and above all their draughts were too deep to enable them to enter the small ports of call that were popular for cruises. Some companies, such as HAL, responded by introducing small ships reserved for tourist-class passengers (the *Rijdam* in 1951 and the *Maasdam* in 1952), and a transatlantic liner with two classes (the *Rotterdam* of 1959, which became the company's flagship) that could easily be converted into a single-class cruise ship by means of an ingenious system of sliding panels.

Although Cunard tried to convince its passengers, in its advertising slogan from 1952, that 'Getting there is half the fun!', and the French Line proclaimed itself 'Your gay entrée to Europe', urging 'Come aboard for all the pleasures of France' and insisting on the pleasures of the table, ships were no longer the only means of intercontinental travel: with the arrival of the Boeing 707, they now faced competition from the jet airliner. In 1957, passengers who crossed the North Atlantic by sea outnumbered those who took the plane for the last time. In the face of the financial problems that were soon to follow, the companies gradually withdrew their ocean liners in order to send them for scrap or devote them exclusively to cruising. Those that escaped the scrapyard were refitted throughout so as to remain attractive to the cruise market: their decks were opened up to the outside, air conditioning was installed throughout, their decorations were updated, and above all their cabins were sold as tourist class.

Many companies that had reigned over the cruise world now disappeared. The necessity for Hapag, which merged with Norddeutscher Lloyd, Cunard White Star, P&O, the Holland American Line and the French Line to find new uses for their ocean liners was made all the more urgent by the appearance of Italian and Greek newcomers such as Homes Lines, Costa Line,

Greek Flotta Lauro Lines and Chandris Line. Specialists hitherto in transporting mail and immigrants to South America, these Mediterranean shipping lines turned to the cruise market in response to the dwindling supply of government contracts. Aged liners, tenders, ferries, cargo boats, Liberty ships and even tankers: for these new operators, any refitted vessel was ripe for a second life as a cruise ship. The SAL's *Kungsholm* and Matson's *Malolo* and *Mariposa* thus became respectively Homes Lines' *Italia, Atlantic* and *Homeric*. Ocean liners of the 1940s to 1960s were destined to sail under many different flags during their careers, as witness the case of the Moore McCormack sister ships *Brazil* and *Argentina*, launched in 1958: after sailing under the HAL colours in the 1970s as the *Volendam* and the *Veedam*, they were chartered to Monarch Cruise Lines in 1975–8 and renamed the *Monarch Sun* and *Monarch Star*, before being sold in the 1990s to Commodore Cruise Lines, who re-baptised them the *Enchanted Sea* and *Enchanted Isle*.

High demand and optimistic forecasts for growth encouraged the new operators to invest in the first generation of modern cruise ships. In 1965 Homes Lines, which two years earlier had become the first company to concentrate exclusively on cruises, launched the *Oceanic*. Designed as both an ocean liner and a cruise ship, she was marketed by Home Lines as 'the largest ship ever designed for year-round cruises', and was the first to be fitted with a 'magrodome', a retractable glass roof covering the whole of the lido deck in bad weather. But innovation was to come above all from European – especially Scandinavian – operators, who were to invest in a new fleet to be based not in Europe but directly in the Caribbean.

Left
With her single deck giving access to all the lounges, the *Eugenio C.* (1966), the last Italian transatlantic liner, was easily converted into a cruise ship – after carrying passengers between Genoa and South America for ten years – by the Costa cruise line in the 1970s. This photograph was taken after 1984, when the ship was renamed the *Eugenio Costa*.

Left
In the 1980s, the popular television series *The Love Boat* was set on the cruise ship *Pacific Princess* (formerly *Sea Venture*). Her sympathetic and efficient crew, under the command of Captain Merill Stubing, contrived through a series of improbable romances to restore their passengers' zest for life.

The Birth of the Modern Cruise

The modern cruise began with the arrival on the scene of new Norwegian and American operators who concentrated on the Caribbean market, operating out of the ports of the American east coast, and who thereby saved the cruise industry from bankruptcy. In 1966, the Norwegian Caribbean Line (NCL) launched the *Sunward*, a ferry that could carry 600 passengers and 500 vehicles. She was followed in 1970 by the Royal Caribbean's *Song of Norway* – with the first glazed restaurant, solarium and wraparound cocktail bar, the iconic Viking Crown Lounge, offering unparalleled views from atop the vessel – and in 1972 by the Royal Viking Line. American operators – Princess Cruises in 1965, Carnival Cruise Lines, 1974 – also launched themselves in this new venture. Carnival Cruise Lines, founded by Ted Arison – former founding partner with Knut U. Kloster of NCL – bought the *Empress of Canada* from Canadian Pacific to turn it into its flagship, *Mardi Gras*, and made Miami into the chief centre of operations for Caribbean cruises. With this first 'fun ship', joined in 1975 by *Carnivale* and in 1978 by *Festivale*, it was the ship itself, with all its many on-board attractions, that became the true destination of cruise passengers.

The objective of these new pioneers was to use relatively low prices to tempt middle-class passengers of all ages on board for cruises of a week, or even a few days, to the eastern Caribbean. Once on board, it was to be hoped that they would spend lavishly. Air travel, hitherto considered as the enemy, was now pressed into the cruise operators' service. Gone was the necessity for long, cold wintry crossings in wild seas to reach the warm waters of the Caribbean or the Mediterranean: now, thanks to NCL's Out Island package, passengers could fly to Florida, San Juan or any other warm water port and embark straight away. This symbiotic relationship with the airliner was to be pushed to its logical conclusion in 1974, when Royal Cruise Line launched the *Golden Odyssey*, designed to accommodate the entire complement of a Boeing 747, or 460 passengers.

Thanks to an aggressive marketing campaign, the cruise gradually became accepted in the United States as a form of vacation like any other. The ABC television sitcom *The Love Boat*, broadcast from 1977 to 1987, was a contributory factor in this success, as one of its stars was none other than the ocean liner *Pacific Princess* of Princess Cruises. Carnival pulled ahead from the other operators at this time, thanks to an innovative and aggressive marketing and advertising strategy, including television commercials in prime-time slots (notably during episodes of *The Love Boat*), television programmes made on board ships of their fleet, and special offers for young people on MTV. To woo travel agents, Carnival offered ten dollars to those who recommended a cruise as first option, and a thousand dollars if this was a Carnival cruise. Once it had established itself as the leading company in the American market, Carnival gradually bought up the smaller companies before taking on the major European operators. Thus in 1989 it acquired the Holland America Line, which had concentrated on cruises since 1973, in 1997 Costa *Croisière*, and in 1998 Cunard. Thanks to the mobility of their fleet and their recent acquisitions, Florida-based operators now cover a large part of the traditional cruise areas.

Right

The *Majesty of the Seas*, last sister ship of the *Sovereign of the Seas*, delivered in 1992 by the Chantiers de l'Atlantique in St Nazaire, is one of the third generation cruise ships of the Royal Caribbean Line. The *Majesty of the Seas* and her sister ships were the first passenger ships to be built on this scale since the *France*.

The Cruise Ship: Prime Cruise Destination

Carefree holidays at sea had become the niche market of the new cruise ship operators. But as the Miami-based operator Carnival was quick to point out, they operate in the vacation industry, not in the cruise industry: 'We're not shipping, we're tourism,' in the words of Mickey Arison – son of Ted Arison, founder of Carnival Cruise Lines – as reported by the maritime historian Gérard Cormier. Interest was now turning away from the traditional model of the cruise and towards Las Vegas and Disney World in Orlando, the two leading American tourist destinations, which served as paradigms for everything from the decorations and size of the ships to the activities offered on board. As Gérard Cornier explains, 'to maintain attractive prices aimed at the middle classes while also keeping their profit margins, cruise operators have competed with each other over the years in the construction of ever bigger cruise ships in order to spread crew, fuel and other costs over a larger number of passengers.' This race for the highest tonnage and the most colossal size began in 1979, when NCL bought the *France*. Modernized, restructured for cruising and refitted, the world's largest transatlantic liner was to be hugely successful as the *Norway*, the world's largest cruise ship.

Not content with modernizing old liners, the operators were now investing in new vessels, veritable floating holiday resorts, which would enable them to develop the mass cruise market. These cruise ships caught up with their predecessors in terms of variety and size, and in addition offered amenities and a level of luxury far superior to those offered by the previous generation. The first prototype of this second generation was the *Tropicale*, launched by Carnival Cruise Line in 1982. This 36,600-tonne vessel can carry over a thousand passengers and 500 crew, and can maintain a speed of 22 knots; its amenities include a large swimming pool with a waterslide and a smaller one in the stern. Its distinctive funnel in the shape of a whale's tail was to become the company emblem. In 1988, the Royal Caribbean Cruise Line's *Sovereign of the Seas*, built at St Nazaire, broke all previous records, at 268 metres long and a gross tonnage of 74,000, with accommodation for 2600 passengers in 1141 cabins, all in the lap of luxury. With her sister ships, *Monarch of the Sea* and later *Majesty of the Seas*, *Sovereign of the Seas* was then the largest cruise ship ever built, with the exception of the *Norway*. Apart from their sheer size, the outstanding feature of this new generation of cruise ships was their internal layout: the central atrium, several decks deep and equipped with glazed lifts, was introduced, and passenger cabins were located as far away as possible from the public spaces in order to guarantee the best possible sound insulation. In a bid to attract fans of this type of tourism in greater numbers, chiefly from the American market, the decorations were freely inspired by fantasy destinations such as Disney World and Las Vegas.

As cruise ships have grown in size, so the attractions and entertainments offered on board have multiplied, with passengers seeking diversion during long stretches out on the open sea in enormous swimming pools with water chutes, mini-golf courses, tennis and basketball courts, jogging tracks, beauty and fitness suites, shopping malls, theatres, cinemas, art galleries, night clubs, casinos and restaurants for every taste and pocket. Etiquette on board these very large cruise vessels is a million miles from the rigidly hidebound conventions of the early years of cruising and transatlantic crossings. Influenced by the cheerful, relaxed patterns of life in the Caribbean, the atmosphere is

Below
Although as recently as the year 2000 a ship of a thousand cabins (or two thousand passengers) was viewed as a giant, the capacity of cruise liners has grown appreciably since. The *Oasis of the Seas* and *Allure of the Seas* – of which the prow is shown here at sea – delivered in 2009 and 2010, measure 365 metres in length and weigh 225,000 tonnes (compared with the 66,000 tonnes of the *France* in 1961), and can accommodate nearly 6300 passengers.

Left
Designed to be a destination in themselves, cruise ships have become floating resorts, with a wide range of leisure activities and sports and impressive amusement parks. The Carnival WaterWorks, the new water park on the *Carnival Fantasy*, features a 'Twister Waterslide over 90 metres long and a 'PowerDrencher'.

easy-going and dress is laid-back. Meals are informal, with every dietary requirement catered for. Whether classic or contemporary, the cruise ship has become, in Alain A. Grenier's phrase, 'a liberating space'.

In 1999, the *Voyager of the Seas* – 137,276 tonnes, 3138 passengers and 1181 crew – offered the first seaborne rock-climbing wall, mounted on the funnel, the first skating rink and the Royal Promenade, a boulevard lined with shops and cafés, four decks high and stretching through the centre of the ship. Other operators followed suit, with ships such as the Italian MSC's *Splendida* and *Fantasia* and NCL's *Norwegian Epic*. With *Oasis of the Seas* and her sister ship *Allure of the Seas*, delivered to CCL in 2009 and 2010, new records were set once more. The vital statistics of these two giants are dizzying: 18 decks high, reaching a maximum height above the water line of 72 metres, 360 and 361 metres long, 47 metres wide, with a tonnage of 220,000 tonnes, and capable of accommodating 6296 'guests' (the word 'passenger' is banned), these colossi of the sea are the largest and most expensive cruise ships ever built. To allow them to pass under bridges, their funnels are telescopic.

Each of these floating amusement parks boasts five swimming pools, a water park, children's theme parks, funfairs, a rock-climbing wall, basketball and volleyball courts, zip wires on both sides of the ship, and vast gardens, the first of their kind at sea, with over 12,000 plants including 62 vines and 56 trees and bamboos, some of them nearly 7.5 metres tall. The principal restaurant on the *Oasis*, the Opus Dining Room, can accommodate over 3000 passengers on three levels at one sitting, while at the same time creating the impression of a French restaurant on land. With facilities such as these, ports of call – when there

are any – tend to become secondary attractions. In any case, the sheer size of the mega-ships means that the number of ports they can enter is limited.

Sailing Away Today

While in 1970 there were some half a million cruise passengers on the high seas, nowadays there are twenty million. To cater for this constantly growing demand, cruise operators now deploy a fleet of 300 ships, ranging from 3000-tonne yachts to 220,000-tonne leviathans carrying 6500 passengers.

But who are today's cruise passengers? Although the majority (63 per cent) are still Americans, Europeans – especially the British, Germans and Spanish – are showing more and more interest. Thanks to them, since 1990 the cruise market has grown by an annual average of 7 per cent. Without becoming a mass market, cruising now appeals to a much broader and younger clientele, and is no longer the exclusive preserve of a closed world of the moneyed and privileged classes, as it was for so many years. Although a luxury market still exists, with high ratios of crew to passengers and exclusive amenities, activities and cuisine, most cruises are now designed to appeal to a clientele of more modest income, a change made possible by the growth in the size of cruise ships.

In a highly fragmented market, cruise operators now offer products to suit most clienteles: 'budget' cruises at modest prices for trips of under a week on ships offering a restricted range of amenities, chiefly in the Mediterranean; very popular 'contemporary' cruises, designed to cater to families with children, offering three to seven days in the Caribbean, Alaska, the Mediterranean or the islands of the Atlantic, on board ever-larger ships with

Opposite
Tourism in Antarctica began to
develop only in the 1960s. After
the signing of the Antarctic Treaty
in 1959, large liners were banished
and the region became a model of
eco-tourism. The photograph shows
the *Crystal Symphony* of Crystal
Cruises of the coast of King
George Island in Antarctica.

Overleaf
'Welcome aboard!': the *Monte
Pascoal* of the Hamburg–Süd line in
Funchal Bay, Madeira, during a cruise
of the western Atlantic (Portugal,
Spain and Morocco) in July 1933.

Left
In the wake the luxury
cruises of the nineteenth
century, the popular cruises
of the 1920s and 30s and the
hunting parties of the 1940s,
50s and 60s, in the twenty-first
century Norway and
especially the Arctic Circle
have seen the development
of a tourism of scientific
exploration, on boats of
modest size. The luxury
expedition ship *Hanseatic*
of Hapag-Lloyd here lies at
anchor in Disko Bay, off the
west coast of Greenland.

brash and colourful decorations; 'premium' cruises aimed at regular cruise passengers, with numerous excursions and explorations, in smaller ships with subtler decorations; and finally 'luxury' cruises, lasting over ten days and stopping off at ports of call that are as important as the (very comprehensive) amenities, with more sophisticated interiors, fewer passengers, more space and many cabins with balconies looking out to sea.

While the most popular cruise destination is now the Caribbean, attracting over half of all cruises, the Mediterranean, where ports of call play a more significant role than elsewhere, has seen an astonishing increase in interest over the past decade, overtaking the Atlantic. Considered as offering the greatest potential for growth in future years, the Mediterranean is attracting the largest operators, who are investing in buying, equipping and managing cruise terminals. The natural and cultural riches of Central and South America also appear promising to companies ever eager for new destinations. Finally, Australasia, the South Pacific, the Middle East, the Persian Gulf, South Africa and the Indian Ocean are rich in promise and are poised to overtake the Caribbean in the years to come. Finally, the '9/11 effect' has encouraged the idea in America of cruising 'at home', leading to major growth in destinations close to the United States – Mexico, Alaska and the Caribbean – and in the increasingly popular cruises specializing in the polar regions, both the Arctic and Antarctica.

Aware of the importance of environmental issues in an ecology as delicate as that of the oceans, cruise operators have begun to consider solutions that will enable them to reduce the ecological impact of their vessels, particularly in the design of the next generation of cruise ships. Already Carnival uses only biodegradable detergents, while Holland America has installed toilets and showers using reduced amounts of water. Some ships are equipped with treatment systems for water and waste, and with installations for reducing CO_2 emissions. The engines of *Oasis of the Seas* are equipped with pollution scrubbers that eliminate SO_2 emissions and reduce CO_2 emissions by 20 per cent; in addition, they consume 25 per cent less fuel than those on slightly smaller ships. Companies must also now take the effects of climate change into account in the structural design of the cruise ships of the future, factoring in increasing numbers of tropical storms, hollow waves and hurricanes in the Caribbean, and a longer high season in the Baltic, among other effects.

Born in the late nineteenth century, organized before the First World War, developed during the 1920s and 30s, doomed in the 1950s and saved in the 1970s, cruising has adapted constantly to changing conditions. Appealing to our love for freedom, imagination and history, it offers an experience that is out of the ordinary and out of time. For all these reasons, its fascination remains as strong as ever.

A MEDITERRANEAN CRUISE de Luxe

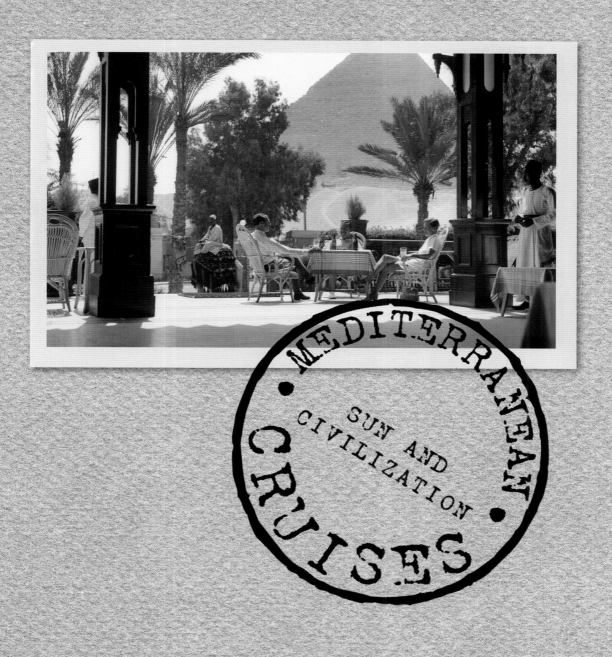

MEDITERRANEAN
CRUISES
SUN AND
CIVILIZATION

Cruising the Mediterranean
Sun and Civilization

A Modern 'Grand Tour'

'The Mediterranean', wrote the historian Fernand Braudel in 1966, 'is ... a thousand different things at once. Not just one landscape, but countless landscapes. Not just one sea, but a succession of seas. Not just one civilization, but several civilizations overlaid on each other ... The Mediterranean is a crossroads of Antiquity. For millennia, everything flowed towards this sea, disrupting and enriching its history.' Surrounded by a number of mountain ranges whose foothills waded out to sea to form peninsulas, capes and large bays favourable to navigation; strewn with islands of all sizes and fringed by many different nations; forming the link and crossroads between three continents and four world cultures (Latin Catholicism, Islam, Judaism and Greek Orthodoxy), the Mediterranean represents the finest cruising waters par excellence. Just as the Mediterranean leads navigators from one cape to the next, so it could be said – to adapt the words of Paul Morand, the French writer and 'traveller through lives and landscapes' who described travel as a modern art de vivre – to lead the cruise passenger from one surprise to the next.

Travelling in the wake of the traditional Grand Tour, the obligatory rite of passage for young British aristocrats, as well as of the 'Oriental journey' of the Romantics and of various pilgrimages, and following the example of the group voyages organized by the first international travel agents – Henry Gaze and Thomas Cook in England; Frank C. Clark, Raymond & Whitcomb and American Express in America – it was to the Mediterranean that the first pleasure cruises gravitated in the late nineteenth century. Rich in a history of tremendous density and complexity, the destinations of the Mediterranean were of capital importance. The climax of the earliest cruises, including the one organized by P&O in 1844 using several of its steamers, was the Pyramids. The destination of the first American pleasure cruise, organized on board the *Quaker City* in 1867 by the Reverend Henry Ward Beecher, meanwhile, was the Holy Land. From the Pillars of Hercules (the Strait of Gibraltar) to the shores of Palestine, an itinerary gradually developed that by the early twentieth century would become a classic: starting from Madeira (Funchal) or the Azores, depending on whether the cruise ship came from the United States

or northern Europe, the cruise would continue via Gibraltar, Algiers, Valletta, Alexandria (Cairo), Jaffa (Jerusalem), Beirut (Damascus), Smyrna (Ephesus), Istanbul, Piraeus (Athens), Venice, Messina and Palermo, Naples (Rome, Venice, Florence), Ajaccio, Genoa or Villefranche (Monte Carlo, Nice, Menton) and Malaga (Granada).

While 'going ashore' nowadays tends to mean a lightning visit of anything from a few hours to a day, ports of call in the golden age of cruising, from 1890 to 1939, were an opportunity for passengers to immerse themselves at leisure on optional excursions. In the early twentieth century, Mediterranean cruises – whether on the *Fürst Bismarck* of Norddeutscher Lloyd, *La Touraine* of the Compagnie Générale Transatlantique or the *Celtic* of the White Star Line – might last for over two months, so permitting the ships to linger for several days in each port of call. Four or five days were set aside for Athens, Constantinople and Jerusalem, a week for Naples and Italy, and no less than twelve days for Egypt and excursions up the Nile. In the 1960s, the Cunard Line's *Caronia* perpetuated this tradition on her spring cruise, which lasted thirty-seven days and followed a virtually unchanged itinerary: Funchal, Gibraltar, Tangier, Valletta, Alexandria, Beirut, Haifa, Piraeus, Catania and Messina, Naples, Villefranche, Barcelona, Malaga, Lisbon, Cherbourg and Southampton.

From Funchal to Algiers: A Gradual Introduction to the Orient

What better way to visit some of these legendary ports of call than in the company of the passengers of the *Fürst Bismarck,* which on 6 February 1894 steamed out of New York to the rousing strains of the *Star-Spangled Banner,* played by the ship's band. Long before the ship entered Mediterranean waters, the cruise had already begun. Six hundred and fifty American passengers, all with Mark Twain's *Innocents Abroad* firmly in their heads, were sailing off on a two-month cruise. Although this NDL cruise liner was one of the most luxurious of the era, the cabins were still small, as William M. Hoyt, a wealthy wholesale grocer from Chicago, observed: 'I will never forget the forlon look of my wife as she took to her room and rolled into her bunk, 2x6, remarking: just think of it, two months on ship-board and such a bed as this.'

CANADIAN PACIFIC

At this time of year, ships almost invariably set sail from New York in the teeth of blizzards and rough seas. Sometimes the vessel would be diverted, especially via Bermuda, in search of better conditions for the Atlantic crossing. It would be at least four days before the passengers could do justice to the meals provided on board. When the ocean was calm, on the other hand, the German liner was so stable that 'one could imagine oneself in the large salon of a continental hotel'. According to another passenger, Edward S. Wilson, life on board was 'fit for a prince'. 'Meals', he went on, 'were served in the most elaborate style and the food was provided with no regard for the expense.'

After a crossing of six to eight days from New York, or four days from Southampton, Plymouth or Hamburg, the cruise ships put into port for a few days in the islands of the North Atlantic. Usually they docked in the Azores or Madeira which – although they lay in the Atlantic, to the west of the Strait of Gibraltar – nevertheless enjoyed a Mediterranean climate. The Madeiran port of Funchal was particularly popular as a foretaste of the exotic things to come, with its lush vegetation and steep, and narrow streets that could be scaled with ease if one were carried on a litter by two men or hauled up on a toboggan behind a pair of oxen. A little cog railway carried tourists up to the village of Monte, from where they could admire the scenery and gaze back on the cruise ship lying at anchor in the harbour, in the very heart of the old town. After a visit to the magnificent botanical gardens, the only way of getting down again was to take a seat in one of the *carros de cesto,* wicker toboggans on wheels, pushed by white-clad *carreros* wearing rubber-soled shoes, which shot down the three kilometres of winding cobbled streets to the harbour. After calling off at the high chalk cliffs of Gibraltar – where the passengers would be amazed to discover that donkeys made up half the living inhabitants – the *Fürst Bismarck* headed for Algiers, and the travellers' first taste of the Orient.

Algiers, the white city upon that passengers could admire through their portholes in the early morning, its houses climbing up the slopes of its amphitheatre of hills, its quaysides and its slopes, all – to American eyes – presenting a suitably picturesque mixture of the Orient and the Occident. While its handsome façades and illuminated shop windows reminded them of Paris, its streets were lined with olive trees, palm trees, willows, cedars and luxuriant orange trees, and the cafés thronged with an exotic mixture of customers wearing the last word in Parisian chic and the burnous, the colourful traditional

MITTELMEERLÄNDER KANARISCHE INSELN
PORTUGAL SPANIEN MAROKKO MALLORCA RIVIERA ÄGYPTEN

FERIENREISEN ZUR SEE
MIT DEN DEUTSCHEN AFRIKA-LINIEN

Arab dress. Only a handful of passengers were brave enough, however, to penetrate the dark, narrow alleyways of the Kasbah. But it was in the Ben Ali and Ben Turki bazaars that they would be initiated into the mysteries of bartering, with its unchanging ritual of an invitation to sit on a stool followed by offers of coffee and cigarettes, accompanied by interminable bargaining and a great show of indifference by the stallholder as he waited for an offer. The skills thus gained would be useful training for the Khan el-Khalili bazaar in Cairo, the Souk el Hamidiyeh in Damascus, or the Grand Bazaar in Istanbul. They would encounter their first 'baksheesh boys' and other beggars, all clamouring endlessly for a few coins, a scene that played out everywhere in the southern Mediterranean. The luckiest of them would be invited to visit the Governor's palace and its gardens, while others would be treated to the languorous mysteries of 'le couché couché', or the belly dance.

After stopping off at Ajaccio to visit Napoleon's birthplace, then at Genoa, where passengers would head off on the train to lose a few dollars at the Casino of Monte Carlo before visiting Nice, the ship would then head off for the most eagerly anticipated ports of call of the whole cruise: Egypt and the Holy Land.

Rendezvous with History

Generally, passengers would wake up gently in the harbour at Alexandria, spotting the Pharos Peninsula and Pompey's Pillar from their cabins. But on the cruise of the *Celtic* in 1902 the seas were rough, and unloading the 400 trunks by barge took such a time that the passengers lost patience. Captain Lindsay decided to lower them one by one into the barge, seated on a chair lashed to ropes. By this unorthodox means it took two hours to winch down 160 of the passengers, while the remainder climbed down the accommodation ladder. When they got to the railway station they found the train had left, and they had to wait twenty-three hours for a special train to take the first 200 passengers, with the rest following on the next one.

After four hours in an 'express train', the passengers of the *Fürst Bismarck* reached Cairo, where they were split up between the city's various hotels. Those who were looking for peace and quiet preferred the two former palaces of Khedive Ismail Pasha, the Gherizeh Palace or Mena House, at the foot of the Pyramids, to the noisy Shepheard's Hotel, the chief advantage of which was its central position. There followed a series of visits, sometimes in freezing weather that took the Americans by surprise and obliged them to huddle in their winter clothes as they toured mosques, universities, Koranic schools

Above
The twenty-five-metre tall pillar of red Aswan granite that greets cruise passengers as they arrive in the port of Alexandria was built in honour of the Emperor Diocletian in the late fourth century. For centuries it served as an aid to navigators. Photograph by Bonfils, late nineteenth century.

Below
River cruise ships in front of the Ptolemaic temple of Kom Ombo, on the banks of the Nile south of Luxor. This excursion was offered during a cruise on the *Celtic* as early as 1902.

Opposite
When this photograph was taken in the 1920s, climbing the Great Pyramid at Giza – more tiring than difficult and now no longer permitted – cost a few shillings and was extremely popular with tourists. The summit of the Great Pyramid was so densely covered with graffiti that, according to the *Usborne Illustrated Guide,* 'it was difficult for the newcomer to find a clear spot in which to write his name'.

Inset: Cover by Anton Ottomar of a Hamburg–Süd brochure for 1935.

On board the Monte Pascoal

The five new Monte class cruise liners of the Hamburg–Süd line – built
to the same design between 1924 and 1930 and named after South American
mountains – sailed on South American routes, notably carrying emigrants to
Brazil and Argentina. It was on these ships that the German line inaugurated
its 'popular' cruises at moderate prices. The *Monte Pascoal* was launched in
1930, and from 8 to 29 July that year made her fourth voyage and first
pleasure cruise to the threshold of the Mediterranean, with the Azores,
Madeira, Morocco and the Iberian peninsula on the itinerary. This unknown
photographer had eleven Agfa films developed by the Berlin photography
studio Franke & Co on the Kürfurstendam, which belonged to the co-owner
of the German optical goods manufacturer Rollei.

Left to right, top to bottom
Friends and relations wave the *Monte Pascoal* off from the port of Hamburg, on the pontoon built by the shipping line to the east of St Pauli Landungsbrücken (St Pauli landing stages) and reached via the Überseebrücke footbridge.

Sunshine and striped deckchairs on the top deck create the perfect condition for a spot of *dolce far niente*.

Jaunty tunes from the ship's band on the promenade deck.

The *Monte Pascoal* lying at anchor in Funchal harbour, Madeira, the first port of call on this cruise.

Those who managed to avoid the *bomboteiros* who climbed on board as soon as the ship arrived in Funchal Bay to sell embroideries and work by local craftsmen were not allowed to leave without a souvenir of the island.

Left to right, top to bottom

On the black sands of Praia Formosa, west of Funchal.

Disembarking at Casablanca, where buses are waiting to take the German passengers to Rabat.

Visiting the Andalusian gardens of the fortified Kasbah of the Udayas, built by the Almohads at Rabat.

Crowds on rue Souika, leading from Rabat harbour into the medina, viewed from above.

An appearance on the Mechouar – to an admiring and astonished audience of passengers from the *Monte Pascoal* – by Prince Moulay Hassan Ben el-Mehdi, Caliph of Tetouan.

Left to right, top to bottom
A souvenir photograph of the ship, on the open seas between Tangiers and Andalusia.

In the ornate gardens of the Alcazar, Seville.

Tea time in Seville with traditional Andalusian *mantecados,* under the amused gaze of some young locals.

The extravagant red and ochre fairytale palace of La Pena in Sintra, Portugal.

Officers of the *Monte Pascoal* leaving Lisbon on the return voyage to Hamburg.

and museums of antiquities and went on excursions to Memphis and Sakkarah and cruises up the Nile. Whenever parties of tourists arrived at the foot of the Pyramids pandemonium would break out, with street children truing to attract attention with shouts of 'Good Melikan gentleman!' and 'Yankee Doodle come to town!' and demanding 'baksheesh' before offering them any service at all. Their valuable experience in Algiers notwithstanding, passengers did not always manage to grasp the rules of bargaining Egyptian-style: sometimes the sellers of scarab amulets would run after them, demanding to be paid a second time, and the scene might even descend into blows. As the *Fürst Bismarck* steamed off towards Jaffa, its next port of call, a rumour spread throughout the ship: a doctor from Buffalo, it was said, had brought a young Egyptian girl on board by force, and now held her confined in the ship's hold without food. An indignant delegation of passengers confronted the doctor, demanding an explanation. 'I fear it is now too late,' he explained to them. 'Food would not do the girl any good – she has already been dead three thousand years.' The doctor had bought a mummy in order to present it to the Buffalo Medical Society, of which he was president.

Disembarking at Jaffa, the port of Jerusalem, was always a tricky business. Lined with reefs just below the water level, the coast was more or less constantly battered by violent surf that obliged large vessels to drop anchor out at sea. To reach land, the passengers had to leap from the accommodation ladder into large boats, supported with great difficulty by the oarsmen. On the return, it was not unusual for the passengers to have to wait several hours for the sea to calm down before they could get back to their ship. The journey on to the Holy City was by train; the passengers found everything dirty, but were soon caught up in the biblical atmosphere. Divided up into groups, they set off on excursions to the high spots of the Old and New Testament: Jerusalem, Bethlehem, Jericho and Nazareth. They were accompanied by 'dragomans' – guide-interpreters in Syrian dress, often Christians or Jews who spoke Turkish, Hebrew, Arabic, French and English – and a small escort armed with sabres and pistols. They walked on the Mount of Olives, swam in the Dead Sea and filled little bottles with water from the River Jordan, while crowds of half-submerged Russian pilgrims were baptized by a priest. On the cruise of the *Celtic* in 1902, the Freemasons' lodge that had formed on board ship met several times in Zedekiah's Cave, also known as Solomon's Quarries. Accommodated in modest hotels, monasteries or large encampments of numbered tents, the passengers often found that the meals they were served on land were less lavish affairs than those on board.

From Constantinople to Athens

After calling at Smyrna – notable for its visit to the Temple of Artemis at Ephesus, where disappointed passengers would discover that all that remained of this wonder of the ancient world was a few ruins – the steamer entered the Dardanelles before heading for the Sea of Marmara. The arrival of cruise ships at Constantinople, which became Istanbul in 1930, was 'a godsend for the Orient', generally heralded by a rise in prices. 'What else could relieve these congested stalls – these rows of riches brought from Persia, India and the islands?' wondered William M. Hoyt in 1894. An inquisitive crowd gathered at Galata port to watch as the passengers disembarked from the *Fürst Bismarck*. The allocation of the horse-drawn carriages waiting on the quayside caused an altercation between the rival companies of Thomas Cook and Henry Gaze that came close to descending into fisticuffs. 'One side, it was alleged, had engaged a certain number, which the other side had bought off by higher offers; hence the muddle, over which controversy a large portion of Constantinople's population presided with abounding curiosity.'

After visiting Hagia Sophia – where the capacious slippers they had to wear over their boots were always in danger of slipping off – the tourists went their separate ways in the city, which with its painted wooden houses appeared to them rickety, moth-eaten and antiquated. The massive traffic jams mingling ox-drawn carts, horses, donkeys, dogs and pedestrians wearing the traditional fez were a source of fascination, notably because of the packs of wild dogs – half-wolf, half-jackal and covered in scars – that formed the city's sub-population and seemed to live in perfect harmony with the human population, serving as their refuse collectors and fire-watchers. Passengers armed with letters of introduction would head for the palace of Ahmed Ali Pasha, head of protocol, or for the former Topkapi Palace to admire the imperial treasure of precious stones, jewels, antique arms and armour, clocks and optical instruments. With two crates of cigarettes and sweets – gifts from the Sultan – stowed safely on board, the *Fürst Bismarck* then sailed for Greece.

Below left
The third Galata Bridge, spanning the Golden Horn at Constantinople, rested on twenty-four pontoons and was built by a British company. At fixed times, the crowded traffic that crossed it for a modest fee was halted to allow tugs to open up a section so that ships could pass through. Photochrome, c.1900.

Opposite
Album of a Greek cruise in 1923 by the American photographer and globe-trotter Frank G. Carpenter. These photographs show 'where passengers are brought ashore' at Piraeus; a visit to the Parthenon; and an *evzone* outside the royal palace in Athens, which in 1929 became the Hellenic parliament.

Inset: Brochure cover for one of the long spring cruises in the Mediterranean (8 March to 27 April 1960) offered by the Swedish SAL line, on board the luxury ship *Gripsholm* (1957) with its design that was at once Italian and Scandinavian.

Overleaf
Passengers on deck 13 of the *MSC Poesia*, named by Sophia Loren in 2008, rush to the starboard rail for a view of Piazza San Marco. To attempt to limit the *moto ondosa* (wave motion) that causes erosion of the foundations of the buildings of Venice, UNESCO has called for restrictions on cruise line traffic in the Basin of San Marco – within a hundred metres of the Palazzo Ducale – and the Lagoon.

1476. Where passengers are brought ashore in
small rowboats from the big liners in the
harbour of Pireaus.

Further wonders lay in store in Athens, which was reached from Piraeus via a steam railway, an electric railway or a toll road. The passengers of the *Fürst Bismarck* were as entranced by the modern appearance of the city – with its broad, tarred roads equipped with street lighting, its tall marble buildings, its Academy and its handsomely dressed inhabitants, the men all sporting the fez – as they were by the Schliemann Collection or the buildings of the Acropolis (the 'Gibraltar of Athens'), which they generally visited under a blazing sun. The Greek royal family was generous in issuing permits to visit its palaces and gardens, and often honoured British and American passengers by boarding their cruise ships to greet them.

Naples, the 'Pompeian Dances' and Vesuvius

In Naples, after ports of call at Messina and Palermo, cruise passengers received a double shock to their senses, both olfactory and visual, the general consensus being that the city was 'more attractive when viewed from the sea than from the interior'. Although they were happy to visit its Baroque churches and aquarium, Antiquity was the real attraction: they went by train to Pompeii, and on their return to Naples visited the Archeological Museum to see its displays of finds from excavations. Those who were in the know would ask furtively, burying their noses in their Baedekers, for tickets to the Gabinetto Segreto, open to the public since 1860, hoping to 'get a good eyeful' of its oil lamps in the form of winged penises and its erotic frescoes and sculptures. Taking advantage of the tourists' fascination with the risqué frescoes and graffiti of Pompeii and Herculaneum, street hawkers in the 1920s peddled mediocre reproductions of the 'best scenes'. Evelyn Waugh reported that the passengers of the *Stella Polaris* were 'persecuted' by taxi drivers offering forbidden pleasures: 'Well then, you want a see Pompeian dances. Glass house. All-a-girls naked. Vair artistic, vair smutty, vair French.'

Left
During a cruise in 1951, a passenger returns to the *Oronsay*, of the Orient Line, moored in the cruise terminal at Naples, opened in 1936.

Inset: Luggage label, 1940s.

Opposite
According to the 1896 Baedeker, 'The Ascent of Vesuvius is unquestionably an excursion of extreme interest, though not unattended with fatigue …

The ascent is most interesting when the mountain "works", or ejects scoriae and ashes, a condition indicated by smoke during the day and a reflection of fire at night.' This coloured glass plate by Branson DeCou (between 1929 and 1938) shows a tourist who has doubtless arrived on the funicular observing the volcanic activity.

G.ᵗᵒ HOTEL **VITTORIA** NAPOLI

The most intrepid of the party would scale the black, snow-capped slopes of Mount Vesuvius, topped by a plume of smoke that hung over the Bay of Naples. In 1884, as a small group of passengers from the *Ceylon* who had ventured to the rim of the crater prepared to climb down again, disappointed at find the depths hidden by a swirling cloud of the smoke that belched forth, a shower of glowing lava fragments exploded from the depths, as Surgeon-General William Munro reported: 'Some fell back into the crater, some between us, and others far beyond the place where we were standing; one fell at my feet, another hit one of my companions on the arm, happily without harming him.'

Naples was also the starting point for numerous railway excursions to Rome, Florence and Venice, the last of which could also be reached by boat from Ragusa. For passengers on the *Fürst Bismarck*, Naples also signalled a parting of the ways, as most of them had opted to tour the capital cities of Europe under their own steam and would sail back to America on a scheduled crossing from Southampton later in the season.

Only a hundred or so passengers boarded again at Genoa to sail back to New York. Once the ship had rounded the Punta de Tarifa, on the third day out of Italy, it headed into choppy waters, as described by Edward S. Wilson: 'The cooks and stewards performed to empty houses. *Soupes royales, fritures d'agneau, chapons rôtis, chou rouge, haricots beurre, compote, tartes Tivoly, artichauts, loup de mer* and *glaces* followed one another with all the care, abundance and military precision of the early days.' The indisposed passengers preferred to stay out on deck, facing the waves wrapped in blankets and nibbling ginger biscuits, or to lie in their cabins chewing on raw onions. The wealth of memories they had accumulated during their ten weeks in the Mediterranean now vied with the anticipation of reaching home waters once more.

Previous pages
In spring 1935, the Hapag cruise ship *Milwaukee* dropped anchor off Port Said, at the entrance to the Suez Canal, during one of her Mediterranean cruises departing from Genoa. Built in 1929, the vessel sailed the Europe-Canada route before being repainted in white in 1934; after a refit in 1935 she was reserved exclusively for cruises.

Inset: Brochure for the last Oriental cruise by the *Milwaukee*, in 1939.

Right and below
Tourists at the Alabaster Sphinx of Memphis, discovered in 1912, considered one of the most beautiful of the Egyptian sphinxes.

A group of tourists setting off from the Mena House Hotel on camel back to visit the Great Pyramids, c.1933.

Inset: Luggage label from the legendary hotel at the foot of the pyramids at Giza, c.1900.

Opposite
'All the Greek temples of the Acropolis together would look like miniatures beside Karnak,' exclaimed a passenger on the *Grosser Kurfüst* in 1909. Osirid statues of Ramses III in the first courtyard of the Great Temple of Amun.

Split – Panorama

Pages 78–9
The comfortably appointed encampment laid out by the tour operator Thomas Cook at El Habis in Jordan, near the Roman temple of Qasr al-Bint Firaun – the only stone-built monument still standing in the region – for the optional excursion to Petra.

Previous pages
The elegant and futuristic *Splendida*, of the Italian MSC line, with 18 decks and 1637 cabins, at sea off the island of Stromboli.

Above and right
Pages from a photograph album of an Adriatic cruise in the 1920s: the town of Split, Croatia, formerly Spalato in the kingdom of Dalmatia, part of the Austro-Hungarian empire until 1918. The belvedere on Mount Marjan, reached by a long stairway, affords tourists a panorama over the town, including the harbour, the Riva, the palace and the cathedral bell tower. Inspired by the Piazza San Marco in Venice, Split's Republic Square is flanked by the Procuraties – buildings in neo-Renaissance style that formerly housed municipal services – and looks out to sea.

Split-Obala

Inset: Luggage label from the Grand
Hotel Imperial, the first modern hotel
in Dubrovnik (formerly Ragusa),
opened in 1897.

SCANDINAVIAN CRUISES

• THE BIG CHILL •

Cruises to Scandinavia and the Poles
The Big Chill

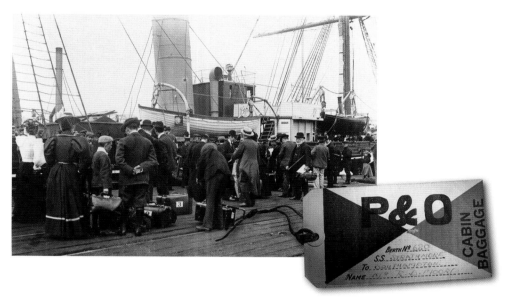

'Just Like Kaiser Wilhelm II'

From the mid-nineteenth century, in the summer months saw aficionados of nature at its most thrillingly untamed drawn in increasing numbers to the deep waters of the Norwegian fjords. With the development of an internal road network, maritime coastal services and finally the railway, and with the creation in January 1868 of the Norwegian Trekking Association (Den Norske Turistforening) to 'foster and facilitate the tourist life in Norway', with similar groups in towns such as Trondheim and Stavanger, Norway gradually opened up to tourism. The first 'organized' visits were British affairs: in 1875, the Thomas Cook agency arranged its first cruise there, chartering the small steamer *President Christie* to permit a score of privileged passengers to admire the midnight sun at the North Cape. In 1884, the P&O steamer *Ceylon*, which in 1881 had been sold to John Clark and turned into a cruise ship for the Ocean Steam Yachting Company, made one of its first cruises in 'northern latitudes'; and in June 1889, the Orient Steam Navigation Company, generally known as the Orient Line, organized its first Scandinavian cruise on the *Chimborazo*.

By the end of the nineteenth century, Norway had become a standard destination for summer cruises. This was thanks to Kaiser Wilhelm II, whose fondness for the wild landscapes of Scandinavia rapidly spread through the aristocracy and upper middle classes of Europe. Up until 1914 he would spend every summer cruising Scandinavian waters, and particularly the Norwegian fjords, on board his large and dazzlingly white yacht *Hohenzollern II*, launched in 1893 from her home port of Kiel. In all, he undertook twenty-six of these Nordic cruises, or *Nordlandfahrten*. Taking advantage of this new vogue, the German shipping lines – including Hapag from 1894, sailing from Hamburg – offered summer cruises in Norwegian waters, so that passengers could admire the fjords and the midnight sun, and – most important of all – steam past the imperial yacht and salute her. Thus it was that, in the port of Alesund on their way back from Spitsbergen on 19 July 1898, passengers on the first 'floating hotel' of the Hapag line, the *Auguste Victoria* (decked out with bunting for the occasion), were granted the honour of welcoming His Majesty aboard, and the privilege of themselves visiting

the imperial yacht, in groups of thirty or forty, to the accompaniment of the ship's orchestra. Until the 1920s, these luxury voyages to Norway remained the exclusive preserve of the seriously rich: in 1908, a cruise to Spitsbergen might cost 1200 marks, the equivalent of half the annual salary of a qualified workman. Not until the mid-1920s and especially the 1930s did the German shipping lines begin to offer fixed-rate cruises on board cruise ships able to carry between five hundred and a thousand passengers, so enabling groups of travellers of more modest means to discover the beauties of Norway.

Alarums and Excursions

The placid waters of the fjords were far removed from those of the North Sea, where navigation could be perilous at any season. This was especially so in the Skagerrak strait linking the North Sea and the Kattegat which led to the Baltic Sea. In May 1896, the *Général Chanzy* of the Compagnie Générale Transatlantique, sailing from Oslo (then Christiania) to Helsingor en route for Russia and the coronation of Tsar Nicholas II in Moscow, hit a terrible storm. One of the passengers on board, Henry Raguet, left an account if this alarming experience: 'The violent slamming of doors, the desperate ringing of electric bells, the disturbing crash of breaking glass and porcelain, the thud of bags torn from their place and thrown violently against the cabin walls, the waves slamming against the portholes, the sinister creaking of wooden panelling and the vessel's structure with each violent juddering of the ship – all this kept us awake throughout the night. Add to this the fact that we had to fight with all our might to against the rhythmical battering caused by the ship's rolling, and to spend hours – in order not to be flung out of our bunks – clinging now to any bumps on the wall, now to the wooden bed frame, a not inconsiderable gymnastic feat, and you may begin to understand the momentary rush of excitement we felt on reaching land at Helsingor at six o'clock the next morning.'

After surviving these testing waters, navigating the maze of islands that protected the Scandinavian coast against rough seas, in clear, calm waters, was certainly more restful for the passengers, but remained just as stressful for the crew. 'This navigation so filled with attractions is one of the most perilous and complex in the world,' explained Jules Leclerc, who in 1903 cruised to Spitsbergen on board the *Oihonna* – a Finland Steamship Company vessel that usually sailed on the Stockholm–St Petersburg route – with 45 passengers on board, 37 of them German. 'The pilot remains on the bridge

Above
Passengers on the *Kungsholm*, of the SAL, admiring the snow-covered peaks on a cruise to the North Cape in 1939. Hamburg–Süd label from the 1930s.

Opposite
Out at sea, on the sun deck of the Hapag ship *Oceana*, which cruised to Norway from 1894. After the First World War, the Hamburg-based German line did not resume its Scandinavian cruises until 1927 with the *Reliance*.

day and night, holding our destinies in his hands, or rather in his lynx-like eyes.' However experienced steamer captains might be, once they came within sight of the Scandinavian coastline they hoisted the flag requesting Norwegian pilots and look-outs to come on board, preferring to allow these seasoned hands to take over and steer the ship through the channels between the countless reefs and islands off the jagged Norwegian coast, serrated with inlets and fjords. Guiding the *Oihonna* was the man who normally piloted the imperial yacht. Occasionally, in regions where few soundings had been taken, a depth-sounding vessel would sail in front of the steamer.

Thanks to these precautions, accidents were rare. In one of the earliest and most serious incidents, which took place in 1906, the *Ile-de-France* of the SGTM ran aground during a cruise to Spitsbergen that had been organized in conjunction with the *Revue générale des science*. Although he had two Norwegian pilots, and at Tromsø had taken on an ice pilot experienced in navigating the polar regions, the captain – lulled into a false sense of security by the fine weather conditions and lack of sea ice – had decided to push further north, heading for Raudfjorden. But in the early morning the ship ran aground on a rock near the fjord entrance. Despite fruitless attempts to lighten it by dumping its coal stocks overboard, the steamer began to list dangerously with the tide, and the 150 French passengers were put ashore, with a little food and water, on Outer Norway Island. Spotted by Theodor Lerner, a German journalist and adventurer on board a nearby whaling ship, the passengers were saved and the stricken ship was refloated before being towed off by the *Friesland*, a Dutch cruiser. On their return to Paris, the grateful passengers presented their saviour with a gold pocket chronometer.

Even nowadays, despite the assistance of electronic navigation instruments, this hostile environment is not without its perils. In June 1989, the Russian cruise ship *Maxim Gorki* ploughed into an ice floe in thick fog and – gashed in two places below the Plimsoll line – nearly sank. The 575 passengers on board, mostly West Germans, and a third of the 379 Russian crew were evacuated in orderly fashion into the lifeboats, before being winched to safety by helicopter a few hours later or escorted to the Spitsbergen archipelago by the Norwegian coastguard vessel *Senja*. Then they were flown home.

Itineraries of Majestic Beauty

Most Norwegian cruises sailed up the west coast to the North Cape, a journey which took on average sixteen to twenty days. Thanks to the effects of the Gulf Stream, Norwegian ports, even at extreme latitudes, were ice-free throughout the year. The most visited area remained the stretch of coast between

Opposite

The luxury ice-breaker *Kapitan Khlebnikov*, converted in 1994 for cruises in extreme conditions and chartered by the American tour operator Quark Expeditions, was one of the first ships to offer cruises departing from Spitsbergen via the Russian High Arctic, as well as a navigation of the North-West Passage, between the Arctic islands of the Canadian North. This was also the first vessel to offer a circumnavigation of the Antarctic to passengers, in 1997.

Right

Hunters from the former whaling station of Smeerenburg, at the north-western point of Spitsbergen, in a scene that would have been familiar to cruise passengers in the region in the late nineteenth century (photochrome, c.1900).

Inset: Luggage label from an Arctic cruise on the Bergen & Newcastle Line, c.1920.

Cruising Scandinavia with the Hamburg–American Line (Hapag)

Around 1905, Hapag published an album of photographs of its three-week-long Scandinavian cruises *(Nordlandfahrten)*, featuring ports of call and excursions including Odde, Bergen, Alesund, Molde, Drontheim, Geirangerfjord, Naes, Merok, Oie, Loen, Blaholmen, Sognefjord, Gudvangen and Stalheim.
The photographs also show the liners used for these cruises until 1914: the *Auguste Victoria*, the first European liner with twin screws; the *Prinzessin Victoria Luise* (which sank off Jamaica in 1906); and the *Oceana, Meteor* and *Blücher*.
The leather album cover, embossed in 'Viking' style, was made in the workshop of the Hamburg bookbinder and leather worker Georg Hulbe (1851–1917).

Clockwise from top left.

The cruise sailed for Iceland from Edinburgh.

Visit on horseback to the Gullfoss waterfall near Reykjavik, Iceland.

Passengers from the *Blücher* wait to board the tender on the shore of Advent Bay in Spitsbergen.

The quay at Hammerfest, the world's most northerly town, at above 70 degrees of latitude.

The town of Tromsø.

Clockwise from top left
At Tromsø, the *Prinzessin Victoria Luise* goes to meet another vessel, possibly Wilhelm II's yacht.

The *Prinzessin Victoria Luise* at anchor at Naes in the Romsdalsfjord.

An excursion to Stalheim sets off from Gudvangen in horse-drawn carriages.

The *Auguste Victoria* viewed from the Norwegian coast.

Passengers board a tender to return to the *Meteor* after a visit to the village of Merok, in the Geirangerfjord.

Clockwise from top left
The Stalheim Hotel, opened in 1882 twelve kilometres west of Gudvangen, at the head of the Nærøyfjord.

The *Meteor* in port at Bergen.

Souvenir photograph in front of the terminal moraine of the Kjendalsbreen glacier near Loen, in the Nordfjord.

The *Meteor* in the Geirangerfjord.

Hotels at Odde in the Hardangerfjord.

Overleaf
The *MSC Orchestra*, of the Italian line MSC Cruises, lying at anchor in the Geirangerfjord in Norway. With the Nærøyfjord, this majestic fjord became a UNESCO World Heritage Site in 2005.

NORDLANDFAHRTEN

HAMBURG-AMERIKA LINIE

FERIENREISEN im SOMMER 1934
MIT DER HAMBURG-SÜD VON RM 160.— AN
HAMBURG-SÜDAMERIKANISCHE DAMPFSCHIFFFAHRTS-GESELLSCHAFT

Bergen and Trondheim, with majestic fjords –including the Hardangerfjord, Sognefjord, Nordfjord, Storfjord and Moldefjord – whose snow-capped peaks, reaching up to 1000 metres, were reflected in the glittering deep green waters and their malachite depths. Some cruise lines allowed passengers to leave the ship in one place and rejoin it in another, making the journey by horse-drawn carriage, train or motor car. Thus it was possible to disembark at Oye, on the Norangsfjord, and to cross the mountains by sleigh before rejoining the ship at Hellesylt on the majestic Geirangerfjord, celebrated as the epitome of Norwegian beauty. As the number of horse-drawn vehicles and motor cars was limited, this excursion had to be reserved on booking. When Hamburg–Süd cruise ships docked at Bergen, it was not unusual to see a hundred motor cars and two hundred horse-drawn carriages waiting on the quayside for the passengers who had reserved them. In the 1930s, the Hapag cruise ship *Oceana* even offered scenic flights on board the seaplane she carried. While standard cruises took in only the southern fjords, other more specialized itineraries headed north to the Arctic Circle. These were major voyages, taking in Scotland, Iceland and Spitsbergen, and could last for over thirty days.

As the steamers penetrated ever further north, so the seascapes and landscapes became yet more majestic. From September to mid-April, passengers could stand on deck and gaze at the aurora borealis, or northern lights. After passing the southern point of Hestmandö, vessels steamed into the Arctic Circle, and the Svartisen Glacier came into view. As cruise ships entered the Arctic Circle, at 66° 33' S, all the passengers would take part in a special ceremony. Presided over by King Neptune, under whose trident neophytes had to pass before being sprinkled with icy water, the ceremony culminated in the awarding of a diploma certifying the crossing. At Tromsø, dubbed the 'Paris of the North', the midnight sun meant there was no need for any municipal illuminations in summer. In the Tromsdal valley, there was always an excursion to a 'Lapp encampment', where a number of Sami families from the Swedish far north lived during the summer months, with a few reindeer that they displayed to the tourists while selling them utensils carved from reindeer bone. For many years, cruise passengers heading for the far north would buy warm clothes here (including leather or sheepskin jackets, felt waterproofs and wolf skins) as well as fur hats (Russian shapkas, fishermen's caps, caps with ear flaps, balaclavas, fur toques or sou'westers) and sealskin boots, for which they would be grateful as they

Above left
Just disembarked from the *Monte Olivia*, of the Hamburg–Süd line, at Gudvangen on her maiden cruise in July 1927, these passengers are about to set off up the Nærøy valley to the Stalheimskleiva, the road to Stalheim that snakes vertiginously up the mountainside, in order to admire the waterfalls at Stalheim and Sivel.

Above and inset
A Hapag poster by Albert Fuss (1931) and a Hamburg–Süd poster by Ottomar Anton (1934).

Opposite
The *Braemar*, of Fred Olsen Cruises, a Norwegian line founded in 1848, lying at anchor near Flåm, deep in the Aurlandsfjord. This is a branch of the Sognefjord, deep and 204 kilometres long.

NORWEGENFAHRTEN
1914
1.FAHRT 13 Juni-30 Juni   3 FAHRT 24 Juli-7 August
2   "   4 Juli-21 Juli   11. Aug.-25. Aug.

NORDDEUTSCHER LLOYD BREMEN

Opposite
Page from a photograph album kept by a passenger on a Norwegian cruise on board the *Atlantis*, of the Royal Mail Line, in August 1930. The visit to the Lapp summer encampment at Lyngen, near Tromsø, was organized for the tourists, according to Jules Leclerq, by 'some agent of the Tomas Cook company'. Below, passengers celebrate their ascent of the North Cape around the small obelisk commemorating the visit of Oscar II, raising a toast not in the traditional champagne but in beer. As early as 1898, Charles Robot observed wryly, 'Today the North Cape has become one of the world's bottle dumps.'

Inset: Stamp advertising a forthcoming NDL cruise in 1914, designed by Otto Amtsberg. Meeting the indigenous Sami people, who added an exotic touch, was a high point of the scandinavian cruises.

Right
The northern lights or aurora borealis over the village of Nyksund, on the Vesterålen archipelago in Norway.

steamed through the ice floes. One of the highlights of the cruise was the North Cape, the final destination of many itineraries. Although it is not in fact the most northerly point in Europe – which lies 1.5 kilometres further north at Knivskjelodden – the North Cape, with its looming sheer black cliffs, was indisputably more impressive. Before 1956, when a road was built allowing access by bus from Honnigvaag, passengers would be put ashore on the southern shore of the island, before setting off to trek through the mountains for hours to reach the plateau. In the 1880s a walkway was constructed from Hornvik Bay to the east, consisting partly of a path and partly of steps (some eight thousand of them), and lined by a cable stretched between iron posts to serve as a handrail. After a challenging climb that took an hour and a half (covering 307 metres at a gradient of 45 degrees), intrepid climbers would be rewarded with a breathtaking view. During the cruise of the *Auguste Victoria* in July 1898, the climb took place mostly in a blizzard and a mere hundred out of 360 volunteers managed to get to the top. By the time they reached the granite monument commemorating the visit in 1873 of Oscar II, King of Norway and Sweden, some of them, fortified by champagne, found it was all a bit of a blur. Whatever the case, all of them were repaid for their efforts by the extraordinary spectacle of the midnight sun over the Arctic Ocean, and duly received a certificate. Those who had dropped by the wayside or stayed on the shore or on board ship still saw their postcards stamped and postmarked by the newly opened North Cape post office: between them that day, indeed, the four hundred passengers of the *Auguste Victoria* sent no fewer than four thousand postcards.

Onward to the Far North

Two days after leaving the North Cape, the appearance of the island of Bjornoya, or Bear Island, heralded the southernmost point of the Svalbard ('cold waters' in Norwegian) archipelago, which the explorer Fridtjof Nansen described as the 'threshold to the great ice cathedral of Nature'. Sometimes the ice would reach further south than usual, as in the summer of 1907, when the P&O's luxurious *Vectis*, halfway through a cruise, was unable to penetrate further than 74° 30' N. Unless Spitsbergen was the sole destination, five days were generally allowed for the exploration of this archipelago lying

within a thousand kilometres of the North Pole. According to the weather conditions, passengers were put ashore in Sassen Bay, Virgo Bay or Baie de la Madeleine, and visited Smeerenburg, with its tombs and whalebones dating to the seventeenth century, and Longyearbyen, a mining village founded in 1906 by the American John Munroe Longyear, who had disembarked at Baie de la Recherche during a family cruise on the *Auguste Victoria* in 1901. Those who wanted to could go on hunting expeditions, either on land (for reindeer, blue foxes, seals, walrus, petrels and eider ducks) or sea (for whales), in return for a supplement to cover the hire of horses, tents, guns, guides and a whaling boat and crew. On board the *Ile-de-France*, taxidermists were poised to stuff the dead beasts as the cruise continued. The other passengers could visit the coal mines and the remains of the various explorers' base camps. A visit to a whaling station on the Grosfjorden was one of the high points of the cruise. The cruise lines and travel agencies did not spare their clients: after visiting cod drying plants in Iceland and at Hammerfest in Norway, here they had to squelch in boots through 'dreadfully slimy, spongy matter', with a grandstand view of the process by which great whales were cut to shreds using a large iron chain uncoiled from a capstan. Here was the melancholy explanation for the absence of whales on their journey. From as early as the beginning of the twentieth century, passengers complained of no longer seeing whales, or their distinctive spouts rising from the waters off the coast of Finnmark, in Norway's far north. The only whales they had been able to see were the skeletons preserved in the museum at Tromsø. Hunted out of these waters, the great creatures had sought refuge in the waters of Greenland, Spitsbergen and the Baffin Sea.

Above left
A cruise ship in a frozen fjord of the Svalbard archipelago in the polar evening light.

Above
The former P&O liner *Rome*, converted into a cruise yacht and renamed the *Vectis*, leaving London in 1904 for her first cruise of the Norwegian fjords. Until 1912, this was the only P&O vessel to make an annual trip to Spitsbergen, on cruises lasting twenty-eight days.

Opposite
The *Lafayette*, of the CGT, penetrating the pack ice of Spitsbergen on a cruise in the mid-1930s. When the *Cuba*, the line's other cruise ship devoted to Norwegian summer cruises, made her first cruise to Spitsbergen in the summer of 1931, the pack ice was so dense that the vessel was forced to stop, before inching forward with infinite care in order to safeguard her propellers.

EXPOSÉ DE L'ESCALE

À

BERGEN

Arrivée à Bergen samedi 24 août à midi.

Départ de l'excursion à 14 heures : Visite en auto de la ville et des environs suivant programme imprimé de l'Agence Bennett.

"L'Albertville" quittera Bergen à 22 heures.

Vendredi 23 août 1935

OVERZICHT VAN HET OPONTHOUD

TE

BERGEN

Aankomst te Bergen Zaterdag 24 Augustus om 12 uur 's middags.

Vertrek van den uitstap om 14 uur : Bezoek per auto der stad en omgeving volgens gedrukt programma van het Agentschap Bennett.

De " Albertville " zal Bergen om 22 uur verlaten.

Vrijdag 23 Augustus

Marché aux poissons pris

4003 Bergen ved fiskebryggen.

Arrivée à Bergen, le samedi, 2 Août

La ville
s'étend sur
les hauteurs
rocheuses qui
entourent son
grand port.
Vue superbe
à l'arrivée et
au départ

1762. BERGEN. FLÖIBANEN   ATELIER K.K. BERGEN.

HOTEL BRISTOL
BERGEN/NORW.

Maisons en bois hanséatiques

Voyez les belles
NORVÉGIENNES

C. BRANDT
Fondé 1852 BERGEN Fondé 1852

AGENCE DE VOYAGES BENNETT
VISITE
AU
CAMP LAPPON
1 PERSON

Ceci n'est qu'un billet de contrôle,
qui n'a pas de valeur monétaire.
S'il n'a pas été enlevé par le
contrôle, il peut-être détruit.
S.S "Albertville"
No. 1026

BENNETT
selskaber
omobil
e Auto (1 Pers.)
seneur) & Retur
& Retour

"Albertville"
No. 1026

Avenue longeant
le port ; maisons
en bois

Une rue de Bergen

Le port

Fot. Normann.

4026 Bergen – Tyskebryggen.   Fot. Normann.

Previous pages
The lively town of Bergen, formerly a member of the Hanseatic League and the great fishing port and market of northern Europe, was a popular port of call for its shops and picturesque houses. This album was made by a passenger on a cruise of 10–30 August 1935 on the *Albertville*, a ship of the Compagnie Maritime Belge chartered by the tour operator Bennett.

DOPPELSCHRAUBEN-MOTORSCHIFF
„MONTE CERVANTES"
NORDLANDREISE 1929

Montag, den 26. August 1929

Speisenfolge

Frühstück von 7—8 und 8—9 Uhr
Kaffee, Tee, Milch
Gekochte Eier oder Rühreier
Hafergrütze in Milch

Mittagessen um 12 und 13 Uhr
Holländische Suppe
Kraftbrühe mit Gemüse
Schweinskarbonade, Teufelssoße,
Kartoffeln, Wachsbohnensalat
Kalifornische Apfelsinen

Kaffee um 15,30 und 16 Uhr
Kaffee, Tee — Gefüllter Bienenstich

Abendessen um 19 und 20 Uhr
Frankfurter Würstchen, Sauerkraut, Kartoffelmus
Verschiedener Aufschnitt
Butter — Käse
Tee

Above and left
Hamburg–Süd cruises offered fairly basic German fare, as may be gleaned from the menu for 26 August 1929 on board the *Monte Cervantes*. The cruises offered to the Germans by the Nazi organization 'Strength through Joy' from 1934 to 1939 were noted for their etiquette-free, classless ambience.

Opposite
This menu for a Norwegian dinner organized by the Bennett tour company on the *Albertville* in 1935 – featuring such delicacies as 'pickled seagulls' feet' and 'penguin wing with polar rice', with side dishes of jellyfish or whale ('according to size') – is perhaps to be taken with a pinch of salt.

Overleaf
In the nineteenth century the city of Tromsø, on the narrow island of Tromsøya inside the Arctic Circle, was so cosmopolitan in its population that it was dubbed the 'Paris of the North' (a name some claim was inspired by the elegance of the wives of its ocean-going captains). Today it boasts the highest concentration of traditional wooden houses in Norway. Tromsø has always been the point of departure for polar expeditions.

Pages 110–11
Crossing the Arctic Circle, with a certificate to prove it, provides an excuse – like crossing the Equator – for organizing a colourful 'ceremony'. Page from an album kept by a passenger on board the *Monte Cervantes* in the summer of 1926.

Pages 112–13
The midnight sun over the North Cape, silhouetting the terrestrial globe erected there in 1978. Passengers today disembark at Honningsvåg and continue to the North Cape by coach. Once there, a long walk over the Arctic peaks and cliffs is now an integral part of the trip.

Inset: A certificate for visiting the North Cape, issued in the 1920s.

Diner Norvégien

Suggestion du chef
du Camp lapon

Museaux de phoque   Pattes de goéland à l'escavêche

Pâté de foie de morue   Loup-phoque gratiné

Hors cadre : Baleine, selon grosseur

Méduses en belle vue

Spécialité laponne

Cuisseau d'ours blanc, sauce boréale

ou

Contrefilet de renne à la daube

Aileron de pingouin au riz polaire

Glace du Pôle

Banquises en tablettes

Harengs confits

WIVEX

Pous

R

17 Août 1935

POLAR-TAUFE

auf 66° 32' 30"

an Bord des Großmotorschiffes

„Monte Cervantes"

———— ❦ ————

Neptun

Heute morgen wurde mir von meinen Spähern, den Delphinen, die Botschaft gebracht, daß sich ein dampferähnlicher Kahn in langsamer Fahrt meiner Reichsgrenze nähere. Wie mir weiter berichtet wurde, soll dieser Kahn eine recht vielseitige Fracht an Bord haben — Landratten, männliche und weibliche, die die Absicht haben, in mein Gebiet einzudringen und nach Spitzbergen vorzudringen. Aber das geht nicht so ohne weiteres. Da habe ich — Neptun, der Beherrscher sämtlicher Meere und sonstiger wässeriger Dinge — noch ein ernstes Wort mitzureden. Keiner darf ohne meine Erlaubnis die Reichsgrenze überschreiten. Wehe ihm, wenn er es dennoch tut! Und viele Jahre Führung und fortgesetzter Lebenswandel müssen vorausgehen zur Erlangung der Einreiseerlaubnis. Wer diese Bedingungen erfüllt und es verdient, in meinem Reiche Aufnahme zu finden, der wird von mir mit meinem ... getauft und ...

erst ...
ich en...
freue m...
begrüßen...
Euch? Ha...
Huld und ...
und der Ma...
schon, seid h...

Als Zeich...
entschlossen, me...
zu verleihen und ...
orden 1. Klasse mit ...

Und nun zu E...
nennt! Ihr seid ja ei...

Ansprache DES TRITON

der das Nahen des Meergottes Neptun zur POLARKREIS TAUFE vermeldet

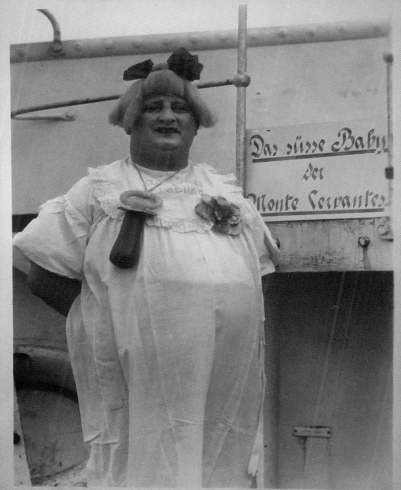

Das süsse Baby
der
Monte Cervantes

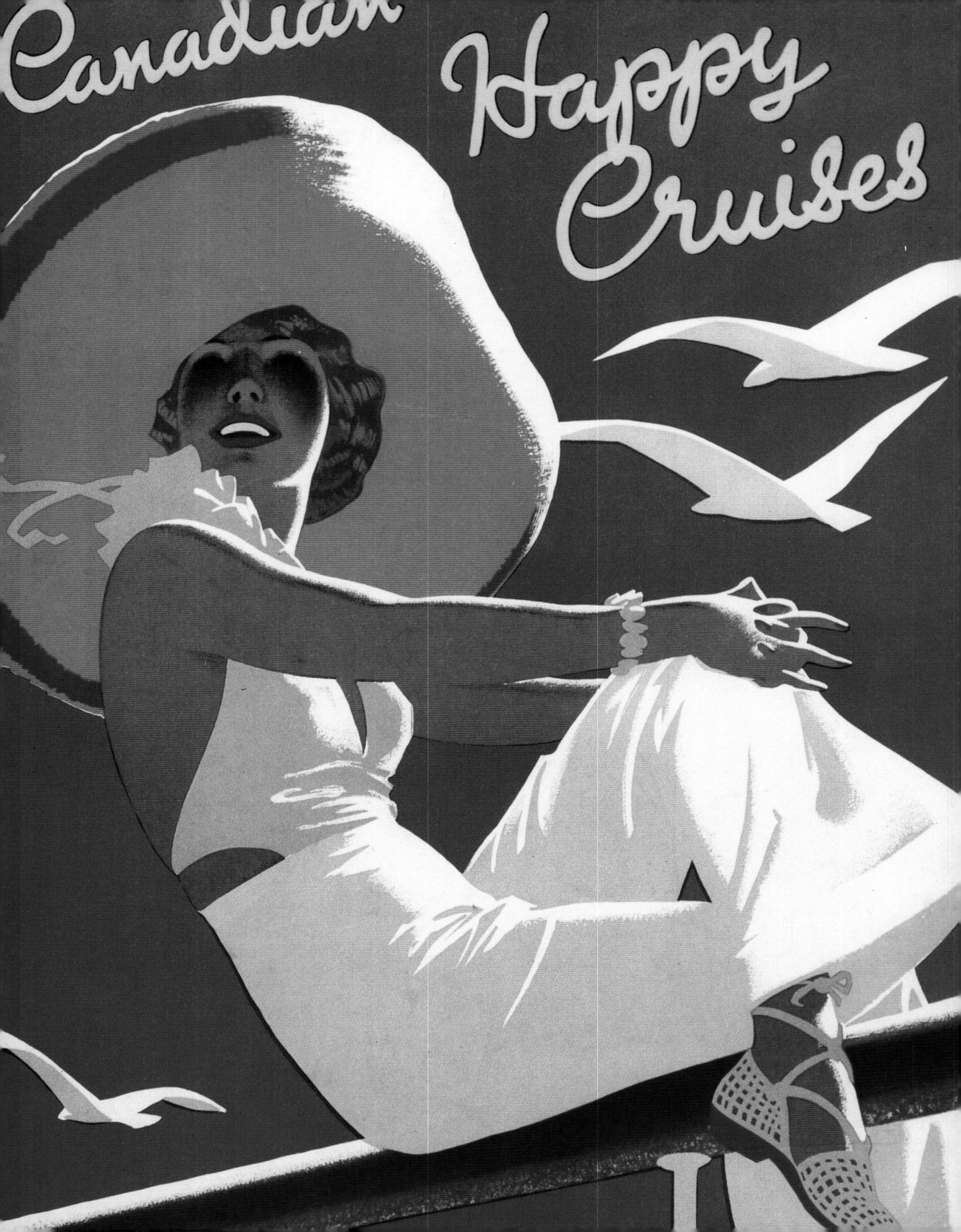
Canadian
Happy
Cruises

The Caribbean Cruise
Voyage to Paradise

Left
Passengers going ashore from the *Reliance* – one of the best-known of the Hapag liners which had cruised the Caribbean since 1896 – during a cruise of the West Indies departing from New York from 2 February to 21 March 1930. The itinerary on the ship's second tropical cruise of the year included Martinique, Barbados, Trinidad, Venezuela, Curaçao, Panama, Jamaica and Cuba.

Previous pages
Glamour and elegance in a poster by Tom Purvis for Canadian Pacific from 1936. The company had entered the cruise business with its 'Empress' steamers in 1922, when it repainted the previously grey and black hulls of its ships in gleaming white.

The famous *Queen of Bermuda* cruising in Bermudan waters close to Fairyland Creek, near Hamilton, in the 1940s.

Opposite
The *Emerald Princess*, of Princess Cruise Lines, lying at anchor in the Bahamas, celebrated for their white sandy beaches, lush tropical greenery, turquoise lagoons and coral reefs. From 1977, the US television series Love Boat was filmed on two ships belonging to this line, the *Sea Venture* and *Island Venture*, renamed *Island Princess* and *Pacific Princess*. Founded in 1965, the line was bought out by P&O in 1974 and purchased by Carnival in 2003.

Gateway to Romance and Freedom

On 19 August 1939, the *Columbus* of the Norddeutscher Lloyd line (NDL), carrying 750 passengers, virtually all American, and 579 crew, all German, on a voyage to paradise – twelve days in the Caribbean – sailed from Manhattan Pier 86. The ship gleamed in its NDL livery of black hull, white decks and sandy-yellow funnels, the ship's orchestra played *Muss I Denn, Muss I Denn zum Städtele Hinaus*, the traditional song of farewell whenever a German ship leaves its home part, and no one could possibly have imagined that this forty-second Caribbean cruise by the *Columbus* would be her last in peacetime, and her last sailing ever. The third largest of postwar Germany's transatlantic liners, the *Columbus* had built up a solid reputation: in 1930 she had completed NDL's first world cruise, and since 1933 she had offered sumptuous winter and Easter cruises, sometimes chartered, in the Caribbean. She thus carried on a tradition started some three decades earlier, by the transatlantic liners that had taken to wintering in these temperate waters that were forever linked with tales of the French corsairs, Dutch freebooters and British privateers and pirates, all of whom had plundered the coastlines and ravaged the Spanish possessions in the West Indies. Caribbean cruises were occasional events before 1914, but developed in the 1920s, notably in response to Prohibition. This prompted many wealthy Americans to go on 'booze cruises' on foreign ships, taking advantage of the opportunity to drink their fill once in international waters, while also visiting the British overseas territories of Bermuda and the Bahamas, or spending a while in the luxury playground of Havana. For the American humorist George Ade, who had cruised the world's seas, there was simply no competition: 'I had a month in the West Indies last Spring on the *California* [of the Anchor Line] and enjoyed every minute of it,' he wrote to a friend in October 1926. 'It was my seventh cruise to the West Indies. It is the best 30-day trip in the world.'

Although nowadays cruises of a week, or three or four days, seem to be the rule in the Caribbean, in earlier days the different cruise lines offered a choice not only in the selection and number of ports of call, the time of year of departure and the length of the cruise (which was never less than a week), but also in the nationality of the ship. In 1912, Hapag offered three cruises lasting for between sixteen

Left

The *Poesia*, launched in 2008 and the third of the 'Classe Musica' ships of the Italian MSC line, formerly Lauro Lines, sailing out of New York on her way to Fort Lauderdale and another Caribbean season. New York, traditionally the port of registry for transatlantic liners and shipping companies, was for many years the point of departure for cruises to the West Indies. In the 1960s, its place was usurped by Florida, which was closer to the cruising zone. The New York Passenger Ship Terminal (also known as Luxury Liner Row) still lies on Manhattan's West Side, at the historic Piers 88, 90 and 92. Two new terminals have opened: the Cape Liberty Cruise Port in Bayonne, New Jersey, used by the RCCL; and the Brooklyn Cruise Terminal [sic] in Red Hook, built to accommodate the *Queen Mary 2* and the Carnival fleet.

Above and left

From 1947 until the late 1960s, the Alcoa company, which imported bauxite from Surinam, offered sixteen-day Caribbean cruises from New Orleans and Mobile on board its three cargo ships, as advertised in this leaflet from 1962.

From 1917 until 1970, Grace Line, which shipped freight and goods between the United States and South America, offered Caribbean cruises that became an important part of its business. This label is from around 1950.

and twenty-eight days; twenty-five years later, in the winter of 1937–8, the *Columbus* offered a total of seven cruises departing from New York, lasting for between eight and nineteen days. That same season, Canadian Pacific was selling four cruises from New York on board its Empress-class ships, of ten, fourteen or seventeen days. The cruises often took in the whole Caribbean, with an itinerary that had become standard since the first cruises of the Hapag vessels *Moltke*, *Meteor*, *Blücher* and *Victoria Luise*: New York, Bermuda, Saint Thomas, Saint Pierre and Fort-de-France (Martinique), Bridgetown (Barbados), Le Brea Point and Port of Spain (Trinidad), Puerto Cabello and La Guaira (Venezuela), Colon and the Panama Canal, Kingston (Jamaica), San Juan (Puerto Rico), Havana (Cuba) and back to New York, making a total distance of nearly eleven thousand kilometres, not counting excursions on land. Give or take a few ports of call, this was the itinerary the *Columbus* was to follow in the summer of 1939, as the storm clouds of war gathered over the heads of its passengers.

Seeking the Sun

Within two or three days of leaving wintry New York, the wind would generally ease, the sea would become calmer and temperatures would rise as the cruise ships headed south. With their home port only a few hours away, its blizzards and storms would be only a distant memory. The other side of the Gulf Stream, the colour of the sea would change from green to deepest blue, while cotton-wool clouds scudded across an equally blue sky. As the weather became warmer, even hot, passengers would venture out of their cabins to spend their days on deck, watching the flying fish. While jackets and ties remained de rigueur for gentleman into the 1950s, warm winter tweeds now gave way to lighter cotton and linen suits. Shorts and swimming costumes were to remain infra dig until the 1960s. The ships' officers, meanwhile, changed into their uniforms: 'The officers appeared in white duck, and the lowest of deck-hands donned a white suit, or at least a straw hat. ... With this official transformation, he who had not brought along at least a white cap and his last year's

Opposite

Caribbean cruise ephemera: leaflet for the Panama Mail Steamship Company (1926–7); menu from a cruise on the Hapag ship *Reliance* (1936); brochure and luggage label from the CGT liner *Antilles* (c.1960); tender timetable for a port of call in Nassau by the *Transylvania* of the Anchor Line (1938); and an advertisement for cruises by the United Fruit Company (1914).

Left

A trio of British passengers sunbathing on the top deck of the *Laconia* during a cruise in the late 1920s.

Above

Two programmes for a West Indian cruise on the *Reliance* in February and March 1930, with excursions to Bridgetown in Barbados and the site of the Battle of San Juan Hill in Cuba, the most crucial battle of the Hispano-American War of 1898.

On Board the Laconia

Album from on board the *Laconia*, which sailed from Southampton or Liverpool in the late 1920s, with ports of call in Madeira (Funchal), Martinique (Saint-Pierre), St Vincent and the Grenadines (Kingstown [sic]), Trinidad, the Panama Canal (Colon), Jamaica (Kingston), Cuba (Havana), Bermuda and the Azores (Ponta Delgada). The *Laconia* entered service between Southampton and New York in May 1922. In November of that year, she made Cunard's first round-the-world cruise, followed that same season by the Hapag's *Resolute* and Canadian Pacific's *Empress of France* and her sister ship the *Samaria*. From 1925, the 20,000-tonne *Laconia*, refitted in more luxurious fashion, made annual winter cruises to the Caribbean, sailing from New York or Liverpool. After sailing on more cruises than scheduled transatlantic crossings for most of the 1930s, the *Laconia* was to meet a tragic end. On 12 September 1942, with 2541 people on board, including a thousand Italian prisoners of war, she was torpedoed by a U-boat, as her predecessor had been in 1917. German U-boat crews disobeyed orders from Hitler in order to come to the aid of nearly eleven hundred survivors.

Reminiscences of a Holiday in the West Indies

Clockwise from top left

As the shores of England receded into the distance, many passengers settled into their deckchairs, well wrapped up in woollen rugs, to read or nap.

Funchal in Madeira, first port of call for the *Laconia* after leaving Liverpool.

After spending four days crossing the Atlantic, passengers made the most of the first rays of tropical sun.

Deck games brought everyone out on deck and helped to pass the time during long crossings.

Descent in *carros de cesto* from the village of Monte, perched on top of the hill overlooking Funchal.

Clockwise from top right
When the ship reached the Lesser Antilles, east of the Caribbean islands, passengers could recline comfortably in their deckchairs and watch the flying fish, silvery creatures the size of herrings that would occasionally find themselves stranded on the promenade deck.

Passengers could not avoid a visit to the frontier town of Colon, founded in 1851 and standing at the Caribbean entrance to the Panama Canal. Dripping in the saturated humidity, they could admire the fine architecture and buy a wide range of luxury products – including, naturally, the perennially modish Panama hats from Ecuador.

Laying bets on 'horseracing' on the top deck.

Visiting the Gatun Locks on the Panama Canal.

As the ship entered Caribbean climes, British passengers swapped their sensible winter tweeds for tropical whites.

Clockwise from top left
Excursion to Kingston, Jamaica, at the foot of the Blue Mountains. There passengers could purchase baskets, hats and all sorts of useless items with which to decorate their mantelpieces on their return, including bamboo vases, table centrepieces fashioned out of silky fibres and tropical plants, mounted shells, coral and aquamarines.

The traditional picnic on the banks of the Wag Water River in Castleton Botanical Garden, Jamaica.

Passengers waiting for the tender to take them back to the *Laconia*.

Cooling off in the small swimming pool made of black oilcloth that was erected daily on the ship's stern and filled with sea water.

Follow my leader through the narrow pathways of the Spanish fort of El Morro, which stands guard over the harbour entrance in Havana.

WINTER SUNSHINE CRUISE
BY ORIENT LINE "ORFORD"
BRITISH WEST INDIES
24 JANUARY — 42 DAYS — FROM 86 GUINEAS

Managers: Anderson, Green & Co., Ltd., 5 Fenchurch Avenue, London, E.C.3
West End Offices: 14 Cockspur Street, S.W.1 & No. 1 Australia House, Strand, W.C.2

Above and above right

Chic *Laconia* passengers in light linen outfits on a shore visit in the winter of 1929. While ladies wore elegantly coordinated costumes and cloche hats, gentlemen had to sport the full panoply of jacket, tie, brogues or correspondent shoes and felt trilby.

Brochure for Cunard Caribbean cruises, 1920s.

Oppositet

The Orient Steam Navigation Company, or Orient Line, whose steamers navigated between Britain and Australia via the Suez and Panama canals, was the originator of the idea of the 'holiday cruise', a concept it formulated as early as 1889. Robert Gibbings' poster from 1935 is an invitation to indolence and winter sunshine on board the *Orford* – which conformed to this British company's custom of choosing names for its fleet beginning with 'O', including the *Orcades*, *Otranto*, *Ormonde*, *Oronsay*, *Orama*, *Orontes* and *Orion*.

summer suit presented a sorry spectacle," wrote William T. Corlett, a passenger on the Hapag's *Oceana* in February 1908. Fortunately the tailors of Charlotte Amalie, Port of Spain or Kingston were able to save the day by running up made-to-measure summer suits within a few hours. But the results could not always be guaranteed, as passengers on the second Caribbean cruise of the *Victoria Luise* in February 1913 were to discover to their cost: the only outing the jackets and trousers made for them at Kingston were to have was to a fancy dress ball on the theme of 'Frumps'.

By the afternoon, shade was hard to find. Transatlantic liners were not designed for such sunny climes, and soon everyone on these pleasure cruises would be drenched in perspiration. When the *Mauretania* sailed on her first West Indian cruise in July 1932, the starched jackets of the officers and cabin boys hung limply in the heat, and the velvet hangings in the lounges became a form of torture. Despite the tropical storms that might be unleashed on the ship at any moment, and invariably when least expected, the heat remained stifling. Before the advent of air conditioning, initially in the public rooms and later in the cabins, attempting to sleep inside a hull that had been scorched white hot by the sun and battered by the vibrations of the water throughout the day was nothing less than an endurance test. Before air conditioning became standard on cruise ships in the 1960s, cabins were aired – though hardly cooled – by means of small manual or electric fans hired from the ship's purser, while mechanically operated air vents provided a trickle of tepid air from outside. For many years, dining rooms were fanned by canvas punkas suspended above each table, great flaps that were pulled to and fro either manually or electrically. 'This great heat is utterly draining: one does nothing but sweat, complaining constantly, "Ah, how hot it is!"' lamented Abbé Huard during a stay in Trinidad in 1903.

Until the advent of the new single-class cruise ships in Caribbean in the 1950s, with more open spaces, air-conditioned promenade decks and internal fittings better adapted to the tropical heat, followed in the 1970s by ships designed specifically for the Caribbean by the new cruise lines, such as the Wallenius Line's *Bohème* and the Royal Caribbean Cruise Line's *Song of Norway*, the passengers' only defences against the sun were shade and darkness. Great canvas awnings were stretched either on a

tracked frame or between posts to extend out over the after deck and so provide passengers with some protection from the sun. Some passengers would hire mattresses and sleep outside on the promenade deck, so as to benefit from the cooler night air; another favoured spot was the top deck, where the canvas sun screen offered shelter from smuts from the funnels and any sudden gusts of rain. On the *Columbus*, young lovers would spend the night in the hatchways, as fourth officer Otto Giese remembered: 'There they had the stars shining above them, while the roll of the ship rocked them gently in a soft, cool breeze. There they exchanged kisses and love promises. But they were rarely alone in their romantic reveries. Every now and then, dark binoculars would appear above the rail of the bridge, scanning the darkness and on the look-out for lovers. Each couple had been secretly spotted by the young officers. And when the watch changed at midnight, the officers would check on their progress.'

During the day, those who were determined to sunbathe no matter what had only to go up on the top deck and stretch out beside the deck swimming pool. The pool on the *Columbus*, one of the first outside pools on a cruise ship, was installed at the front of the ship. Originally consisting of simple collapsible structures of waterproof canvas that were placed temporarily on deck and filled with unheated sea water, deck pools became a permanent feature. In this new space dedicated to idling and sunbathing, with a cool drink to hand, life was organized around wicker deckchairs, sunbeds and parasols in a passable imitation of the sun-soaked terrace of a Roman café – a style raised to a peak of perfection on the *Rex* and *Conte di Savoia* of the Italian Line.

Island Adventures: Between Escapade and Education

Even before land hove into view, tantalizing perfumes and aromas would waft on deck, carried on the sea breeze and bearing the promise of unusual and picturesque discoveries. Every evening, the programme for the following day would be slipped under the cabin doors. 'The printed circulars were assuring, of course, and held out attractions not heretofore offered, but old travelers are wary of excursions of all kinds; so the Columbia professor, the doctor, and myself selected only those which, from our lack of definite data as to trains, we felt compelled to choose in order to be sure of re-embarkation. To be left,

Previous pages
The *Rex*, of the Italian Line, at her moorings in the port of Rio, 10 February 1938. Although she usually sailed the express transatlantic service between Genoa and New York, in December 1932 the *Rex* set off from New York on a Caribbean cruise. She was fitted out with many sumptuous features that made her suitable for pleasure cruises, including two outside swimming pools on her stern, a vast lido, a solarium, courts for badminton and other sports, a gymnasium, a rifle range, a bar with a balcony overlooking the sea, and a spa with massage couches and ultraviolet lamps.

Below left
The covered terrace of the *Seven Seas Mariner*, the small and highly luxurious vessel operated by Regent Seven Seas Cruises and offering all-inclusive gastronomic cruises.

Opposite
The promenade deck of the Hapag cruise ship *Prinzessin Victoria Luise*, c.1900. The sun awning offered protection not only from the heat of the sun's rays but also from tropical rains storms and smuts from the smoke stacks.

Overleaf
The swimming pool on the Laconia was still a temporary first-generation structure of oilcloth slung between wood or steel posts. The first example of this type of pool seems to have appeared on the *Adriatic* of the White Star Line in 1907. It was only in 1926, on the Italian Line's *Roma*, that a permanent outdoor pool was first installed, at the ship's stern. The *Arandora Star* was the first ship to boast a permanent outdoor pool on the well deck.

Inset: Grace Line's small cargo ships – the *Santa Rosa*, *Santa Paula*, *Santa Lucia* and *Santa Elena*, designed by the naval architect William Francis Gibbs – all possessed large tiled swimming pools surrounded by parasols at the aft of the ship, as seen in this leaflet of 1938.

CAREFREE CARIBBEAN

SAILINGS FROM NEW YORK
Every Friday
visiting
CURACAO · VENEZUELA · COLOMBIA
PANAMA · JAMAICA · HAITI

Crusoe-like, on an island with a Carib population is a situation not especially pleasant to contemplate,' observed William T. Corlett wryly in 1908, knowing that Daniel Defoe had shipwrecked his hero on the Caribbean island of Tobago. Tickets for trips on land had to be reserved at the excursions office when the ship set sail, as the number of places was always limited.

For many years, in the absence of any landing jetties in the ports of the Caribbean, going ashore on the islands was not a straightforward matter. Cruise ships were obliged to drop anchor some distance out to sea (a kilometre at Santiago de Cuba), Leaving their passengers to disembark on to dinghies or tenders which then ferried them to shore. A reception committee would be waiting to greet them, often made up of small craft and children who would dive to retrieve coins thrown by passengers on board. Sometimes, as at La Brea on Paria Bay, Trinidad, the landing craft was unable to beach on the gently sloping shoreline, and the passengers had to get their feet wet. 'But', Abbé Huard recounted with relief, 'we were spared this extremity, as the strapping boatman carried us in his arms, one after another, and deposited us on the rocks: it was many years since we had experienced this mode of transport, and this was not the least remarkable episode of our voyage.' But it was soon forgotten amid the 'curious and instructive' visit, after a two-kilometre trek through white-flowered hibiscus bushes and cinnamon and pineapple trees, to the Pitch Lake, a forty-hectare expanse of natural bitumen, its surface soft and cracked under a blistering sun. At this point, their shoes sinking into the sticky tar, some passengers began to regret venturing so far from the ship.

The early days of cruising were not about entertainment, however, but about discovery and education. Passengers on the *Meteor* in 1908 were subjected to a demanding schedule of instructive visits to sugar plantations on St Lucia; banana, pineapple, coffee and tobacco plantations in Cuba; coconut plantations on Saint Croix; a sugar refinery in Puerto Rico; rum distilleries all over the place; lush botanical

Left

The gleaming new *Norwegian Epic* of the Norwegian Caribbean Line is in the same league as the last colossi of the Royal Caribbean International, *Oasis* and *Allure of the Seas*. The third largest cruise ship in the world, with accommodation for nearly 5200 passengers and 1700 crew, she was built in the St Nazaire shipyards and is the largest vessel ever constructed in France. She entered service in June 2010, starting her career in the Caribbean. These very large vessels cannot put passengers ashore on every West Indian island, as some harbours are not deep enough to provide the landing stages they require.

Inset: Passengers going ashore from a British cruise liner in the West Indies, c.1925.

gardens in Jamaica and St Vincent; and the statue and house of the Empress Josephine at Fort-de-France. American tourists, who loved anything sensational, were particularly keen on the ruins of Saint-Pierre in Martinique, destroyed by the eruption of Mount Pelé in May 1902. They even visited one of the two survivors (out of 30,000 people). And in Cuba they combed San Juan Hill for souvenirs of the bloody battle that had taken place there in 1898, during the Spanish-American War.

La Guaira in Venezuela was another eagerly awaited port of call. From the cruise ship, passengers decanted on to trams that rattled through magnificent mountains for two hours, with windows wide open to let in all the smoke and dust, to reach the capital, Caracas. There, for a supplement of a few dollars, those who wished to could spend the night at Miraflores Palace, the sumptuous residence of President Joaquin Crespo. After a lengthy train journey from Caracas to Valencia – featuring no fewer then 86 tunnels and 212 bridges and passing through forests of mahogany, banyan and flamboyant trees – they eventually reached Puerto Cabello, where the ship was waiting to take them on to Panama. The visit to the border town of Colon and the Panama Canal was for many years the high spot of many cruises, even after work on the canal was completed in 1915. Usually the cruise would end in Cuba, which had become a 'tourist mecca'. But passengers on the *Meteor* were only to glimpse Havana from the ship's rail: because the ship had taken on two passengers at Colon, a 'veritable incubator of yellow fever', the port's sanitary officer ordered the captain to hoist the yellow quarantine flag, and prohibited all passengers from setting foot on Cuban soil.

An Unfinished Cruise

The passengers on board the *Columbus* in the summer of 1939, by contrast, had no shortage of time for visiting Havana, the 'Paris of the West Indies'. After an initial port of call at St Thomas, on 22 August, the German cruise ship's troubles began at Saint-Pierre de Martinique. Faced with the threat of war, the French authorities on the island, which was a French department, would not allow the German crew to set foot on land, and when the ship's photographer defied this order he was arrested and accused of espionage. After a brief stop at Bridgetown the following day, the ship headed south, avoiding the British colony of Grenada, where two submarines were supposed to be stationed in one of the bays, and the port of call of La Guiara. Learning, after anchoring off the Dutch port of Willemstad, capital of Curaçao, of a Polish attack on the German frontier, Captain Daehne took the decision to cut the cruise short and return to New York. The following day, he received a coded message ordering the *Columbus* to seek immediate refuge in any Spanish, Italian, Japanese, Russian or Dutch port, upon which he turned the ship round and returned to Curaçao. The passengers, who had not been ashore for four days, were furious at being kept on board. Some were even frightened that the ship would head straight to Germany, and the cruise would end up in a concentration camp. After another attempt to return to New York on 30 August, a second coded message ordered the captain to get rid of his passengers, who had become a nuisance. Hastily ordering the passengers into the lifeboats, he left them at sea off Havana before steaming off for Germany. Pursued by the Royal Navy, the *Columbus* hid in a number of South American ports before being intercepted, on 19 December, by a British destroyer, which ordered the captain to stop. Rather than surrendering his ship, Daehne decided to scuttle her: off the American coast, the crew set fire to her before abandoning ship and being picked up by an American cruiser. The *Columbus* sank within the hour. Her former passengers, abandoned at Havana, managed to get back to Florida by boat a few days later, and then entrained for New York. There the waiting crowd found them in good spirits, delighted with their eventful vacation.

Opposite
Brochure published by the Hapag in 1938 for what was to be the final cruise of the *Columbus*.

Overleaf
The Caribbean meant all the pleasure of sampling local delicacies and buying souvenirs. Here American tourists tuck into coconut and roast chicken at Nassau in the Bahamas in the early twentieth century.

Inset: An Alcoa Line leaflet of 1947 assures passengers that: 'Shopping will be one of the highlights of your trip,' not only because they would find all the products of the Caribbean and Europe, but also because the modest prices were 'so tempting'.

Left
Passengers returning to the *Columbus* after visiting Bridgetown and the Aquatic Club in Barbados (then a British colony), one of the few ports of call on this cruise. The ship's lifeboats were used as tenders to ferry them ashore.

S. S. COLUMBUS
CRUISES...
THE WEST INDIES
NASSAU, PANAMA
and
SOUTH AMERICA

HAMBURG-AMERICAN LINE ★ NORTH GERMAN LLOYD

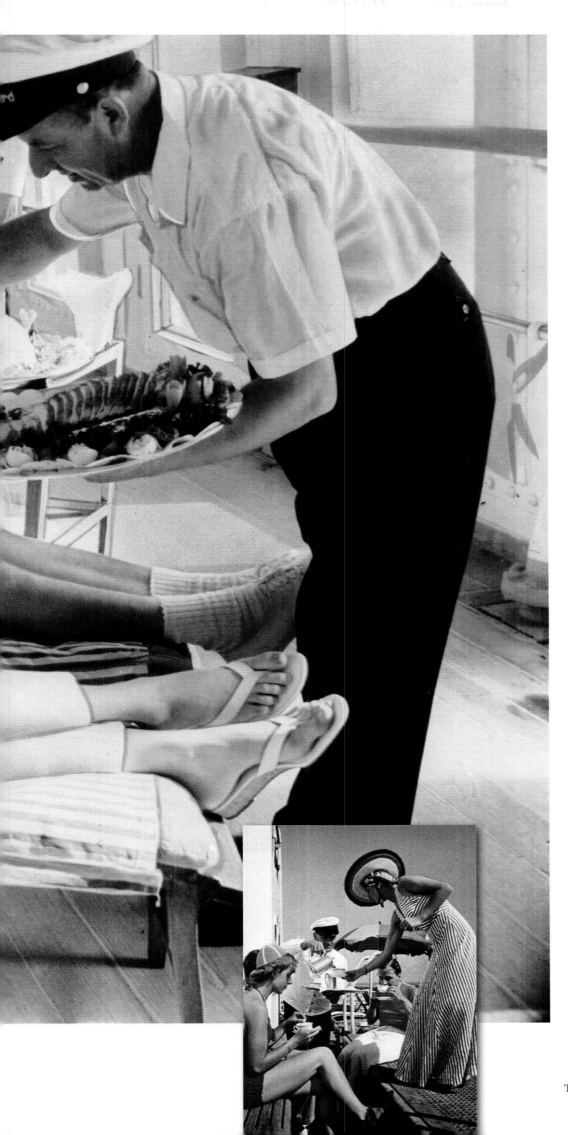

Left

A buffet lunch on deck, on a cruise ship in tropical climes, 1967.

Inset: Tea time on board the Hapag cruise ship *Milwaukee*, c.1938.

Overleaf

Fun and games on cruise liners, from top to bottom: deck tennis on board the *Awatea* (1936); quoits on the *Empress of Australia* (1934); fun in the pool on a White Star liner (c.1930); complimentary pack of cards from the Hapag (c.1935); shuffleboard (c.1930); and horseracing on the deck of the *Laconia* (c.1928).

Page 148

Album from a Caribbean cruise in 1979 on board the Carnival Cruise Line vessel *Carnival*, launched in 1955 as the *Empress of Britain*, one of Canadian Pacific's transatlantic liners, then renamed the *Queen Anna* by the Greek Line in 1964, before being bought by Carnival in 1976. 'Never had a vacation to compare with this – just great,' reads this postcard from 'the fun ship'.

Page 149

The lido and swimming pool on deck 9 of the *Carnival Spirit*, operated by Carnival Cruise Lines. Designed by the marine architect Joe Farcus, responsible for all the American company's ships from 1972, she entered service in 2001. From November to April she cruised the Caribbean, sailing from Miami, then from May to September she cruised Alaskan waters, before repositioning in the Hawaiian archipelago via the Panama Canal. Now based in San Diego, she offers winter cruises on the Mexican Riviera.

Pages 150–1

The court of King Neptune and his wife Amphitrite, a key feature in the famous ceremony of 'crossing the line' (the Equator), on the cargo cruise ship *Brazil* of Moore-McCormack Lines in 1951. Initiates would be baptised in a pool of sea water, before being awarded with a certificate.

Inset: Certificate awarded on board the Hapag liner *Resolute* in March 1933.

the fun ship
tss **Carnivale**
registered in Panama

Never had a vacation
to compare with
this - just great.
We are in Puerto Rico
today - yesterday
Samana. This ship
is like a big floating
hotel. Wish I could
bring our room boy home
with us. Love
Eddi

CARNIVAL CRUISE LINES
820 Biscayne Blvd., Miami, Florida 33132

SAN JUAN, P.R.
PM
22 MAR
1979

Mr. + Mrs. Wenger
6225 N.E. 32nd Ave
Portland, Ore
97211
U.S.A

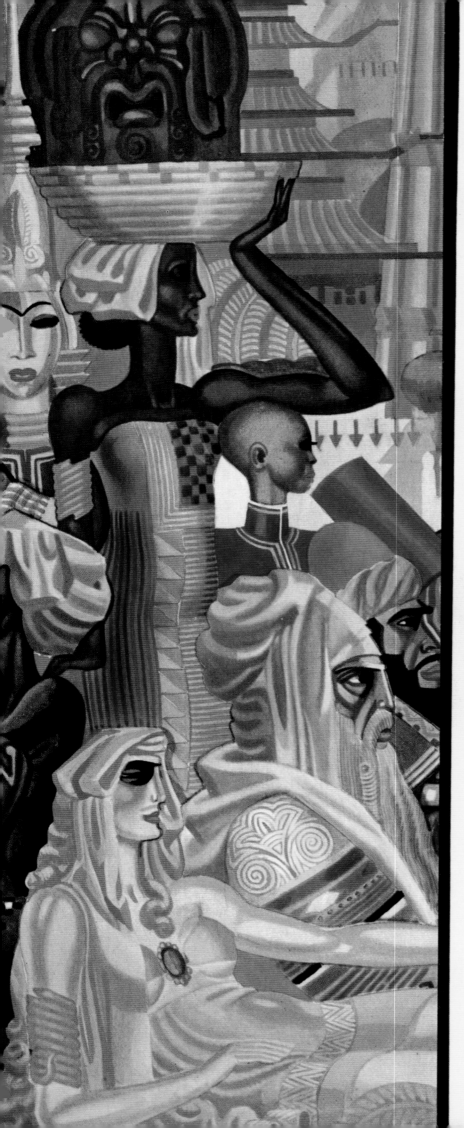

THE

Franconia

1936

AROUND

THE

WORLD

CRUISE

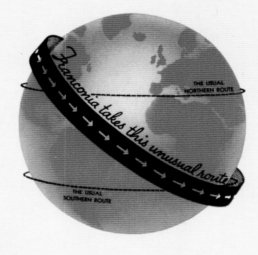

THE USUAL
NORTHERN ROUTE

Franconia takes this unusual route

THE USUAL
SOUTHERN ROUTE

WORLD CRUISES

SAILING
THE GLOBE

World Cruises
Sailing the Globe

At 10.45 on 21 November 1922, 416 passengers waited on Pier 54 of Chelsea Piers, Manhattan West Side, to board the brand-new Cunard liner *Laconia*. Among them was Eleanor Phelps, a young woman from Aiken in South Carolina who was travelling with her mother and sister, and who was aware that she was taking part in an event of some significance: the first circumnavigation of the globe by a cruise ship, with the same port as the point of departure and arrival. For the British Cunard Line this was also, purely and simply, their first world cruise. As every newspaper covering the event knew, the initiative for such a voyage lay with the Hamburg–American Line (Hapag), which had carried out the first attempt at the beginning of the century.

The Cleveland *and the Unfinished World Cruise*

The very first cruise ship designed specifically for this purpose, the luxuriously appointed Hapag steamer *Prinzessin Victoria Luise* (with 160 crew for 180 passengers), was meant to spend 135 days circumnavigating the globe on her maiden voyage in the summer of 1900. But the exorbitant prices charged for the opportunity to join this cruise unleashed a strike in the German naval dockyards, which put paid to the project. After several more failed attempts, scuppered notably by the Russo-Japanese War, it was in the end the American agency Frank C. Clark that succeeded in chartering the Hapag steamer *Cleveland* for the first 'round the world cruise' for 118 wealthy passengers, from 16 October 1909 to 31 January 1910. Advertised as 'princely traveling in balmy climates', this world cruise was in fact incomplete: after leaving New York, the ship crossed the Atlantic and the Mediterranean, passed through the Suez Canal to reach India and the Far East, and returned across the Pacific to San Francisco. In February 1910, the *Cleveland*, with 756 passengers, set sail on a second attempt at a round the world cruise, setting course in the opposite direction and arriving at Hamburg.

As navigation between American ports by foreign shipping lines was forbidden under American law, the Hamburg–American Line was awarded a hefty fine, before eventually having the penalty quashed by the US Attorney General. But the idea had caused a great stir, and the credit was awarded

Left
The painstaking organization of travel arrangements, excursions and accommodation ashore is key to the success of world cruises. This photograph shows members of the *Reisebüro* (travel agency) on board the *Cleveland* during the cruise of 1911–12. 'They work hard to ensure that all goes smoothly, and many of them continue with their duties when they could sneak off and do some sightseeing on their own account,' wrote one appreciative passenger.

to Frank C. Clark himself. George Tom Bush, a passenger on the second cruise, offered ringing praise: 'Mr. Clark did all he could to make everybody as comfortable as possible all through the ship; to take 750 people from their homes all over the United States, nearly every state [and nearly every condition being represented], around the world, land them at the different places, give the carriage, rickshaw and other rides, visiting all points of interest in the places visited as well as many inland trips, keeping them where possible at hotels, the best on shore, providing all the guides etc., and bring all through satisfied was indeed a wonderful undertaking and worthy of great commendation.' Encouraged by this success, repeated in succeeding years, the *Cleveland* thus set the pattern for a winter tradition among shipping lines, prompting the Hapag line to organize similar cruises annually from 1911. With the opening of the Panama Canal in 1915, a genuine round-the-world tour became a possibility. Hapag had it planned: *Cleveland* and *Cincinnati* were to set sail on 30 December 1914 and 14 January 1915 respectively, returning to port five months later – and then, once again, war intervened.

Opposite
A group of passengers from the *Cleveland* visiting the sacred cave of Beten on Enoshima Island in Japan, during the 1913 cruise. Still today the cave is visited by the light of candles or lanterns.

Overleaf
Every week of the year, it was possible to set off on a thrilling round-the-world voyage on board the luxurious President-class ships of Dollar Steamship Lines, sailing from New York, Los Angeles or San Francisco, via Hawaii and the 'sunshine route'. The map shows the round-the-world itinerary offered by this American line in the 1920s. Resting on it are a 'Guest List' of passengers on a cruise in 1932 and a luggage label from the Kyoto Hotel in Kyoto, Japan, opened in 1890.

The Laconia *and the First Round-the-World Cruise*

Chartered by American Express, the *Laconia*, dubbed the 'ship of millionaires' although there were in fact only a handful on board, was to spend eighty days at sea, with another fifty days reserved for tours and excursions on land. Her westward itinerary was to become the classic round-the-world route, for

Right
The hundred-day cruises on the *Cleveland* became so famous that in the spring of 1914, Hapag organized two cruises to run simultaneously a fortnight apart, starting in January 1915 and lasting 135 days, on board the *Cleveland* and her sister ship, the *Cincinnati*. The plan was to be scuppered by the outbreak of the First World War.

EUROPE

ASIA

CASPIAN SEA

BLACK SEA

Vienna

Paris

GENOA

Venice

Constantinople

NICE

Rome

MARSEILLES

Madrid

NAPLES

MEDITERRANEAN SEA

Lisbon

Gibraltar

Algiers

Tunis

To Boston and New York

ALEXANDRIA

PORT SAID

SUEZ CANAL

SUEZ

Cairo

EGYPT

RED SEA

Damascus

Jerusalem

Beirut

Bagdad

Karachi

Indus R.

Delhi

Agra

Cawnpore

Lucknow

Allahabad

Baroda

Nagpur

Benares

Ganges R.

Darjeeling

Calcutta

INDIA

Bombay

Rangoon

Madras

Trichinopoly

Tuticorin

CEYLON

COLOMBO

STEAMSHIP LINE

INDIAN OCEAN

Harbin

Mukden

Vladivostok

Peking

Tientsin

Antung

Seoul

Dairen

Fusan

KOBE

JAPAN

Tokyo

Yokohama

CHINA

Chungking

Hankow

Yangtze R.

Nanking

Pukow

SHANGHAI

Canton

Macao

HONG KONG

Mandalay

MANILA

PHILIPPINE ISLANDS

Bangkok

Saigon

PENANG

SINGAPORE

BORNEO

SUMATRA

Batavia

Surabaya

JAVA

CELEBES

NEW

AUSTRALIA

The Cheerful Dining-Saloon

GUEST LIST

LINES

Practicing Golf Strokes

A Dance in the
Verandah Cafe

KYOTO HOTEL · KYOTO JAPAN

Opposite

'My expectations were high but were so far exceeded that there are no words, no possible means of expression. It is beauty & purity & the most delicate fineness, the white of clouds and lovely lace, the warmth of the inside of a shell, all brought into one perfect ethereal whole. … After dinner [we] went to the Taj and saw it in the starlight, with the stars making a nimbus all about it, and the shadowy reflection in the water making it like fairyland,' enthused Eleanor Phelps in her diary on 15 February 1922, after visiting the Taj Mahal.

Inset: Cover by Norman Fraser in 1938 for the following year's cruise on the *Empress of Britain*.

Right

When they sailed through the Panama Canal on 29 November 1922, passengers on the *Laconia* (inset) dined at the Tivoli, a hotel that was opened in 1907 on a hilltop in Ancon, near Balboa and Panama City. The only luxury hotel in the region, it could accommodate nearly seven hundred guests. Its Ancon turtle soup, fillet of Culebra beef, Brazos Brooks asparagus and Gatún fowl *en pot* were famous; cruise passengers preferred an American menu, however.

a clientele that for a long time was to remain largely American. After visiting Havana and navigating the Panama Canal, the ship would spend ten days steaming to San Francisco, before setting course for Hawaii, and on to Yokohama, with visits to Tokyo, Kyoto and Kobe, and then Korea. From Shanghai, some passengers would travel to Peking before rejoining the ship in Hong Kong, while others would visit Taiwan. The ship then sailed on to Manila, Java, Singapore, Burma and India. Eleanor Phelps chose to go on a railway excursion across India, visiting Calcutta, Darjeeling, Benares – where the train was struck by an outbreak of dysentery that would claim the lives of two elderly lady passengers – Lucknow, Agra, Delhi, Jaipur, Baroda and Bombay, where the *Laconia* was waiting. The vessel then navigated the Suez Canal to reach the Mediterranean, where some passengers travelled up the Nile from Khartoum, while others visited Cairo or Jerusalem. The Winter Palace Hotel at Luxor gave a ball in honour of the *Laconia* passengers staying there, and one lucky young female passenger even managed to tag along with a party of Belgian royalty and visit the tomb of Tutankhamun, discovered only a few months earlier. They all met up again to rejoin the ship at Alexandria, which set her course for Naples (with visits to Herculaneum, Pompeii and the Amalfi coast) and Monte Carlo (for Nice and the Côte d'Azur) before heading for Gibraltar (with a visit to Algeciras), the last port of call before crossing the Atlantic.

In the wake of this success, every year four or five cruise liners – often chartered by American travel agents such as American Express, Frank C. Clark and Raymond Whitcomb, or their British counterparts such as Thomas Cook – offered one or two round-the-world winter cruises of between 80 and 140 days, with between twenty and forty ports of call. The most prestigious of these cruise ships – the Red Star Line's *Belgenland*; the Cunarders *Laconia*, *Samaria* and *Franconia*; Hapag's

AT AMBER

THE PALACE COURT
AMBER

This page
Eleanor Phelps and her mother went by 'auto' to Amber, the abandoned city near Jaipur, before riding up to the fortress on the back of an elephant. 'Until one tries riding an elephant one has not achieved the ultimate in slow locomotion! The sun was hot and we swayed and bumped,' wrote Eleanor of this scene captured in her album on 20 February 1923.

Opposite
Canadian Pacific – which could be said to have invented the world cruise in 1891, when it marketed the maiden crossings of three new liners under delivery as round-the-world cruises – entered the regular world cruise market in 1922, the same year as Cunard. Poster by R. Holling (1924).

OLD CITY OF AMBER

THE MOTOR CAR OF THE EAST

Cruise
to the Gateway Ports round the World

14TH
JANUARY
1925
from NEW YORK

Canadian Pacific

Resolute and *Reliance*; Canadian Pacific's *Empress of France*, *Empress of Britain* and *Empress of Scotland*; SAL's *Kungsholms*; and NDL's *Columbus* and *Bremen* – were to dominate the field throughout the 1920s and 1930s. After the Second World War, many transatlantic liners devoted their old age to world cruises. From the 1960s, the Holland American Line's *Rotterdam* was to undertake twenty-nine legendary world cruises. The French Line's *France* made only two cruises of over four months, in 1972 and 1974, while the QE2 offered twenty-five during her long career. Because of Italy's colonial wars in the 1930s, most cruise liners abandoned the Mediterranean route and instead sailed via South Africa. Ports of call made perilous by the second Sino-Japanese War were replaced by others in Bali, Formosa, Borneo, Somalia and Australia. But Hong Kong remained a staple of the itinerary, and there was no question of missing the Great Wall of China. While these long cruises were barely profitable for the cruise lines – with ships carrying at best half their passenger capacity – they were essential to their prestige.

Five Months on Board

For most passengers, a round-the-world was the experience of a lifetime, and not one that many would have the chance to repeat. Until the 1950s, passengers generally booked for the whole cruise, with only a few (usually friends or relations of existing passengers) joining the ship en route. Today's passengers can choose a leg of cruise, spending upwards of eight nights on board,

Right

Magazine advertisement of 1928 for the sixth world cruise of the Hapag vessel *Resolute*, dubbed the 'Queen of cruising steamships', and a luggage label from the 1930s.

Around the world with the Hamburg–American Line (Hapag)

Following the success of its two first cruises, on the *Cleveland* in 1909 and 1910, Hapag published an album – described as a souvenir but intended as publicity – featuring the iconic ports of call of its cruise ships, the *Prinzessin Victoria Luise,* the *Meteor* and the *Cleveland.* Photographs of the ships' interiors were followed by images of shore visits that covered only part of the itinerary of the first round-the-world cruise: the Mediterranean, the Orient and India. As with the line's earlier albums, the binding was by the Hamburg bookbinder Georg Hulbe.

Clockwise from top left
View of the harbour at
Funchal, Madeira, the first
port of call after leaving
New York.

Strolling in the streets
overlooking the harbour
at Villefranche-sur-Mer.

In harbour at Palermo, Sicily,
beneath Monte Pellegrino.

The *Meteor* steaming past
the Riva degli Schiavoni in
the Venetian Lagoon before
arriving at the Palazzo Ducale
and Piazza San Marco.

View of the port of Naples,
with Monte Pellegrino topped
by Castel Sant'Elmo behind.

Opposite, clockwise from top left

A Montenegrin gun seller, a typical sight in Cattaro (Kotor after 1918), a Venetian city and port in the kingdom of Dalmatia, then part of the Austro-Hungarian empire.

Inhabitants of Corfu taking the air beside the harbour.

In the Holy Land: excursions to the Dead Sea, the lowest point on earth, and the River Jordan, where Jesus was baptized.

The Temple of Edfu, dedicated to the god Horus and the second largest temple in Egypt.

A visit to the Sphinx at Giza, with the site still buried by sand.

The harbour at Constantinople (Istanbul), with behind it the terraced roofs, palaces, towers and minarets of the city, overlooking the Golden Horn.

Left, from top to bottom

The entrance to the Meenakshi Amman Temple, one of India's most visited holy places, in the southern city of Madurai.

One of the entrances to the Elephanta Caves. Hewn from the solid basalt rock between the sixth and eighth centuries, the caves lie on Elephanta Island in the Arabian Sea, ten kilometres east of Bombay.

Passengers from the *Cleveland* watching the ritual bathing of thousands of Hindu pilgrims in the Ganges.

Above

A moment of relaxation at the Mount Lavinia Hotel, on the west coast of Ceylon.

Opposite
On a world cruise distances between ports of call can be considerable, and meal times are eagerly awaited. Here a welcome cup of tea is served on an unidentified cruise liner, c.1960.

Below
It was on board the brand new cargo and passenger ship *Statendam* [sic], designed as tourist class throughout, that the Holland America [sic] Line organized its first round-the-world cruise, departing from New York on 7 January 1958. Along with the main lounge, the games room – with its typically well-upholstered 1950s décor of dusky pink armchairs and fitted carpet – was the most popular public room on the ship.

Inset: Detail of a brochure for this cruise.

Overleaf
Passengers on the *Franconia*, dubbed 'Franconians', sunbathing on the ship's bow after a dip in the pool. This cruise, from 15 January to 31 May 1929, was chartered by Thomas Cook under the command of Captain E.T. Britten.

according to the time and means they have at their disposal. As the maritime historian John Maxtone-Graham recounts entertainingly, hard-liners among the seasoned travellers took a dim view of the new arrivals, accusing them of upsetting the balance of the cruise. Living with the same people for 90 to 130 days was not always easy: ' ... the first month, everyone was very polite and friendly and obviously trying to make a few friends, [generally weighing everybody up]; by the second month, everyone had been sized up by their fellow passengers and they had all made friends ; towards the end of the second month, they were beginning to get on each other's nerves and by the third month, everyone was screaming at everyone else but then, as the end of the cruise drew near, everyone is crying because they don't want to leave each other.'

To ward off boredom during the long sea crossings, the days and evenings were filled with concerts, balls, wooden horse races, card or euchre parties and a wide range of deck games. Passengers rested, read a great deal and informed themselves: reputable speakers would give lectures on the religions and customs of the countries they were about to visit, and would shed light on their politics through topics such as relations between Mussolini and the Pope, Zionism and the Arab world or Indian nationalism. Groups would spring up among the passengers according to their interests or origins: a photography club was able to use a cabin that had been turned into a dark room; a travellers' club met to swap tall tales; passengers from the same American state stuck together; freemasons sought out members of the same lodge; Sons and Daughters of the American Revolution and members of the Society of the Cincinnati organized anniversary celebrations for Washington and Lincoln. On the *Resolute*, some of the female passengers even formed a 'Merry Widows' Club'. And it was not unusual for romance to blossom: on the second cruise of the *Cleveland*, in 1910, a love-struck couple obtained a special dispensation from the Archbishop of Canterbury to be married in London before they sailed back to America. And a widow on the first *Franconia*, Maxtone-Graham records, received a dozen proposals of marriage between New York and San Francisco.

Feeding this small floating town for five months was no small undertaking. In 1924, for 450 passengers and 600 crew, the *Belgenland* took on board 30 tonnes of beef, 9 tonnes of poultry, 6 tonnes of mutton, 3 tonnes of pork, 2 tonnes of veal, 8 tonnes of bacon, 7

tonnes of ham and 70 tonnes of vegetables (60 of which were potatoes), 600 barrels of flour, 4 tonnes of coffee and 5 tonnes of sugar. Fresh fish, vegetables, fruit and ice were taken on board at every port of call. For her cruise in 1932, the *Empress of Britain* stocked up with 3000 bottles of champagne, 3000 of red wine, 2400 of white wine, 3600 of whisky, 69,000 of beer and 32,100 of mineral water. To ensure that none of her passengers should fall ill from drinking the local water, the *Empress of France* carried tanks of New York drinking water, a commodity carried in quantity – 3200 tonnes – by the *Cleveland* as early as 1909.

On Foot or Horseback, by Train or Motor Car

On her world cruise, Eleanor Phelps experienced a bewildering array of modes of travel, including motor car, train (Pullman for night journeys), bus, ferry in Korea, rickshaw in Japan, litter in Hong Kong, dandy-wallah in Darjeeling, palanquin in Canton, horse- or elephant-drawn tonga in Rajasthan, and riding on mules and camels in Egypt. A great variety of visits was organized for travellers who were often eager to learn about and meet the natives, provided that they came from similar worlds. Cigar factories and breweries in Havana, a sugar refinery in Honolulu, a perfumery in Grasse, a camphor factory in Taiwan, botanical gardens, temples and sanctuaries, palaces and even – at Bilibid in Manila – a model prison were all on many of the cruise programmes. Entertainments were also laid on: demonstrations of ju-jitsu in Tokyo and surfing in Hawaii, cockfights in Manila and geisha concerts in Kyoto, not forgetting the casino in Monaco.

Despite the considerable care devoted to the organization of these voyages by the travel agencies and cruise lines, the unexpected always lay just around the corner. The American humorist George Ade described waking to a surprise on a world cruise in December 1928: 'Last Tuesday morning, the 5th, we rose at an early hour and looked out of our port-holes and learned that the big *Belgenland* was crashing her way through floating ice floes. We were many miles out from the port of Chinwangtao. The temperature was just about zero. We peeked out and saw, several miles away, a good-sized steamer trying to break through the ice and get to us. Here was an experience not on

Opposite
Passengers on the 1929 cruise of the *Franconia* getting ready to go ashore from the tender at Paknam, in the estuary of the Chao Phraya River. From there they took the train to Bangkok, some twenty kilometres away.

Inset: Cover of the 1937 *Franconia* brochure.

Below left
At Yokohama, passengers on the *Laconia* discovered a new mode of transport, as decribed by a delighted Eleanor Phelps on 28 December 1922: '...the only sound the plop plop of the coolie's feet in the mud. The men keep up a steady quite rapid jog-trot, so even that you wonder why they don't tire out very quickly. The rickshaws are very comfortable ... & it is a most romantic way of moving.'

Inset: Luggage label from the Imperial Hotel, Tokyo, where the *Laconia* passengers had tea after a visit to the great Buddha of Kamakura. This hotel, designed by Frank Lloyd Wright in 1916, reminded some passengers of the Grand Canyon Hotel at Yellowstone, but was 'more luxurious'.

the program. When we looked over the prospectus of our cruise around the world we did not see any pictures of large steamers fighting their way through ice eight or ten inches thick. We anchored well out in the harbor, and our tender, which was really a tramp steamer of good size, bucked the ice and finally came alongside, but we were hours late in getting ashore, and, oh, what a frigid ride it was from the steamer to the landing.' A very different sort of surprise awaited the passengers on the *Cleveland* in 1910, on their visit to Canton, where a bloody riot had just taken place. Escorted through the narrow streets in groups of ten in Indian file – under an armed guard of two soldiers and two policemen, flanked by signs warning in Chinese that anyone who touched a hair on the Americans' heads would be summarily decapitated, and stared at in silence by the locals – they turned a corner to find themselves in the square where executions took place, where lay the decap-itated corpses of seven or eight river pirates and a woman who had killed her baby.

Happily, passengers were able to recover from their experiences in the western-style comfort of the grandest hotels and palaces, which had been reserved for them throughout the cruise: break-fast at the Cecil Hotel in Delhi; lunch at the Fairmont in San Francisco, the Sevilla in Havana or the Negresco in Nice; tea at Shepheard's in Cairo, the Manila in Manila or the Capuccini at Amalfi; din-ner at Raffles in Singapore, the Winter Palace in Luxor, the Taj Mahal in Bombay or the Moana in Honolulu; or luxury rooms at the Grand in Calcutta or the Imperial in Tokyo. Frequently, however, they found that by far the most comfortable accommodation was to be found on their cruise liner: 'I never was gladder to see anything than I was to see that big comfortable boat, with her ports lighted and clean sheets, soft pillows and the prospect of tubs and a day of rest,' wrote Eleanor Phelps on rediscovering the *Laconia* in Shanghai after spending ten days ashore.

Despite the ordeal of bargaining, which they soon learned to enjoy, and the taxes they had to pay to take their purchases out of the countries they visited, cruise passengers were fanatical shoppers. They accumulated precious stones from Ceylon; embroideries and kimonos, cultured pearls, flower and vegetable seeds, paper and socks from Japan; silk dresses, radios and cameras from Hong Kong; batiks from Java; silks, sandalwood, ivory carvings and lacquered teak boxes from

"IN THE MARKET" MOMBASA

Left
Arab and Indo-Pakistani
traders in the market at
Mombasa in Kenya awaiting
passengers from the *Caronia*,
during her great African
cruise of 12 January to
26 March 1950.

Burma; buffalo-skin fans from Singapore; and copperware from India. When the *Laconia* docked in New York, she was laden with four tonnes of souvenirs. A special storage area under the promenade deck had been set aside for rattan furniture, fabrics and embroideries from Madeira, relics and prayer mats from Egypt, musical instruments and hangings, lacquered furniture and porcelain, ironmongery, household linen and silks, not forgetting the animals of every species – parrots, canaries, monkeys and Chinese chows – that were to be so many living proofs of their new owners' five-star round-the-world adventures.

A dissenting note among all these happy travellers was struck by George Ade, however, whose second world cruise had evidently, as he wrote in 1929, failed to live up to his expectations: 'Last winter I made a cruise around the world. It was supposed to be a pleasure cruise. We were on the same ship for nearly five months, much of the time looking out at a wide expanse of empty water and living on cold-storage food. When you eat certain kinds of food which has [sic] been in the icebox for three or four months it is just the same as trying to eat an inner tube. It tastes like nothing whatever. ... We went up to the north of China where it was 10 below zero. Soon after we were down on the Equator and 120 in the shade. Now, I had been around the world once before and I am still wondering why I went again when I might have gone to Florida ...'

Above
Traditional dolls brought
back by Eleanor Phelps as a
souvenir of her two-day visit to
Korea (then under Japanese
rule) in January 1923.

Opposite
Now as then, cruise
passengers come home with
their suitcases bulging with
souvenirs of their adventures
ashore. Here souvenirs and
bric-à-brac are offered for
sale under the Loggia del
Porcellino in Florence in
the 1930s (photograph by
Branson Decou).

University of California,
Santa Cruz, McHenry Library,
Special Collections

Overleaf
Hawaii, a key destination for
world cruises: booklet from
the Pleasanton Hotel (c.1920),
folding postcards (1935),
and a tourist brochure and
luggage label from the
1930s. Collection Marc Walter

Pleasanton Hotel
PLEASANTON HOTEL
·HONOLULU·T.H.

HONOLULU, T. H.

HAWAII

Greetings from

_____

HAWAIIAN ISLANDS

_____

SUNSET ON DIAMOND HEAD, HONOLULU

The Matson Liner "Lurline" Enters Honolulu Harbor. This is a Sister Ship of the "Monterey" and "Mariposa"

DAVID KAAPUAWAOKAMEHAMEHA AT HIS ONE-MAN HAWAIIAN VILLAGE

...ess to
...any an
...me and
...nship is
...ian styles,
...nty.

...g panoramas,
...eautiful Nuuanu
...pectacles and one
...world.

THE CAPITOL, FORMERLY THE ROYAL PALACE, HONOLULU

Form No. ..-97-C
(150M 65.-757)   PRINTED IN U.S.A.

HONOLUL

STATEROO

Above

A Japanese-themed costume ball: pages from an album kept by a passenger on a cruise in 1935 on the *Chichibu Maru* (1930) of the NYK (Nippon Yusen Kaisha) line. The Japanese line, with its funnel livery of two red stripes, launched its Pacific and world tours in the late 1920s, with a fleet of deluxe new liners, the *Asama Maru*, *Chichibu Maru* and *Tatsuta Maru*. After the Second World War, the NYK never regained its prestige of the 1930s. In the late 1980s, however, it founded a luxury cruise company, Crystal Cruise Line; in 1996, the *Crystal Symphony* sailed on her first world cruise.

Above
Tables were laid out on the promenade deck.

Below
Ladies wearing kimonos bought during their stay in Japan prepare to join their husbands in the main lounge.

Overleaf
The *Silver Cloud* of Silversea Cruises, based in Monaco, lying at anchor here in Halong Bay, Vietnam, is a veteran of the hundred-day world cruise market. Launched in 1994 and designed to accommodate 296 passengers, the ship offers only suites and cabins with sea views, with a level of comfort worthy of a luxury hotel.

Pages 186–7
The *Orion* of the Orient Line sailing from Pier 91B at Pyrmont in Sydney Harbour in the late 1930s, blasting her foghorn under a shower of ribbons and confetti (photograph by Frank Hurley). When she entered service in 1935, this was the first British liner to have air conditioning in all public spaces. Until the outbreak of the Second World War, when she was requisitioned as a troop-carrier, the *Orion* alternated voyages to Australia with occasional cruises departing from England, notably to the Norwegian fjords.

Bibliography

Travellers' tales, guides and brochures

George Ade, *Letters of George Ade*, edited by Terrence Tobin, Purdue University Press, 1998.

M. Baumfeld, *Cruising the Mediterranean; Impressions, and Sketches*, Emil L. Boas, New York, 1905.

René Bazin, *Nord-Sud*, Paris, Calmann-Lévy, 1913.

Carl Beck, *Sonnenblicke vom lateinishen Amerika. Eine Kreuzfahrt nach Westindien, Columbien, Panama und Costa Rica*, Verlag von Leonhard Simion Nf., Berlin, 1908.

George T. Bush, *40 000 miles Around the World, A Personal Narration of the Experiences and Impressions of an Energetic Traveller who Crossed the Equator and the Arctic Circle in the Tour*, Howard Hustler Print, Howard, Pennsylvania, 1911.

Canadian Pacific Railway Company, *Two Mediterranean cruises: Empress of Scotland... Empress of France...*, Canadian Pacific, 1930.

Cook's Cruise to the Mediterranean, the Orient and Bible Lands by the new Hamburg–American Line Twin-Screw Steamship 'Moltke', a 70 day Cruise, leaving New York, Feb. 4. 1903, Thomas Cook & Son, New York, 1902.

William Thomas Corlett, *The American Tropics, Notes from the Log of a Midwinter Cruise*, Burrows Brothers Co., Cleveland, 1908.

Dans le Monde polaire: au Spitzberg et à la Banquise, cruise by the *Revue générale de sciences*, 1906.

T. T. Eaton, *The Cruise of the Kaiserin*, Baptist Book Concern, Louisville, Kentucky, 1903.

Mabel Sarah Emery, *Norway through the Stereoscope; Notes on a Journey through the Land of the Vikings*, Underwood & Underwood, New York, London, 1907.

Edgar Allen Forbes, *Twice Around the World*, Fleming, H. Revell Company, London and Edinburgh, 1912.

William G. Frizell and George H. Greenfield, *Around the World on the Cleveland*, 1910.

Otto Giese and James E. Wise, Jr., *Shooting the War: The Memoir and Photographs of a U-Boat Officer in World War II*, Naval Institute Press, Annapolis, 1994.

John H. Gould, *Grand Winter Cruise of Steamship 'La Touraine' to the Mediterranean, the Orient, and the Holy Land*, Compagnie Générale Transatlantique French Line, Ocean Publishing Company, New York, 1895.

Elias Haffter, *Briefe aus den hohen Norden: Eine Fahrt nach Spitzbergen mit dem HAPAG-Dampfer 'Auguste Viktoria' im Juli 1899*, Frauenfeld, J. Huber, 1900.

Henry Haguet, *Vers le Nord, croisière du Général Chanzy, en Norvège, Danemark, Suède et Russie*, Paris, Chamerot et Renouard, 1896.

W. M. Hoyt, *A Cruise on the Mediterranean or Glimpses of The Old World Through the Eyes of a Business Man of the New*, Pool Bros. Printers, Chicago, 1894.

Abbé Huard, *Impressions d'un passant. Amérique-Europe-Afrique*, Typ. Dussault & Proulx, Québec, 1906.

Robert Urie Jacob, *A Trip to the Orient, The Story of a Mediterranean Cruise*, John C. Winston Co., Philadelphia, 1909.

Jules Leclercq, *Une croisière au Spitzberg sur un yacht polaire*, Paris, Plon, 1904.

R. H. McCready and H. M. Tyndall, *Cruise of the Celtic Around the Mediterranean*, The Winthrop Press, New York City, 1902.

William McFee, *The Gates of Caribbean, The Story of a Great White Fleet Caribbean Cruise*, United Fruit Company, Steamship Service, 1922.

Paul Morand, *De Paris à Tombouctou*, Paris, Flammarion, 1932.

William Munro, *A Two-Month Cruise in the Mediterranean in the Steam-Yacht Ceylon*, Hurst and Blackett Publishers, London, 1884.

James T. Nichols, *Around the World on a Floating Palace*, Nichols Books & Travel Co, University Place Station, Des Moines, Iowa, 1923.

J. C. Oehler, *A Cruise to the Orient*, Presbyterian Committee Publication, Richmond, 1907.

Albert Bigelow Paine, *The Ship-Dwellers. A Story of a Happy Cruise*, Harper & Brothers Publishers, New York, London, 1910.

Eleanor Phelps, *Around the World by the SS Laconia, 1922–1923*, Book I and Book II, Digital Collections, University of South Carolina, Columbia, SC 29208. Available online at: http://digital.tcl.sc.edu/cdm/search/collection/phelps/order/title/ad/asc/cosuppress/0

Quebec Steamship Company, *Bermuda and the West Indies, Winter Trips to the Tropics*, Season 1907–1908, brochure.

Charles Rabot, *Au Cap nord: itinéraires en Norvège, Suède, Finlande*, Paris, Hachette, 1898.

Fernand Robillard, *Croisière en Grèce, en Turquie, Roumanie et Crimée; conférence faite à la Société normande de géographie*, Imprimerie Cagnard, Rouen, 1911.

Pierre Thoreux (commandant), *J'ai commandé 'Normandie'*, Paris, Presses de la Cité, 1963.

Tourist guide to the West Indies Venezuela Isthmus of Panama and Bermuda, Hamburg–America Line, New York, 1909.

Evelyn Waugh, *Labels: A Mediterranean* Journal, Penguin, 1985 (first published 1930).

Edward S. Wilson, *An Oriental Outing: Being a Narrative of a Cruise Along the Mediterranean*, Cranston & Curts, Cincinnati, 1894.

James T. Wilson, *Our Cruise in the Mediterranean*, Lord Baltimore Press, Baltimore, 1899.

Books and articles

Harmut Berghoff, 'Enticement and Deprivation: The Regulation of Consumption in Pre-War Nazi Germany', in *The Politics of Consumption. Material culture and citizenship in Europe and America*, Martin Daunton and Matthew Hilton, 2001.

Marie-Françoise Berneron-Couvenhes, 'La croisière: du luxe au demi-luxe. Le cas des messageries maritimes (1850–1960)', *Entreprises et histoire*, 2007/1, n° 46, pp. 34–55.

John Malcolm Brinnin, *The Sway of the Grand Saloon: A Social History of the North Atlantic* New York, Barnes and Noble, Inc., 1971, new edition 1986.

Gérard Cornier, 'Le paquebot est devenu la destination de la croisière' Du Titanic au Costa Concordia Robin des Bois April 2011. A digital version is available at: http://www.robindesbois.org/dossiers/Titanic/Du-Titanic-au-Costa-Concordia.html

Cruise Tourism, Current Situation and Trends World Tourism Organization, Madrid, 2010.

François Desgrandchamps and Catherine Donzel, *Cuisine à bord, les plus beaux voyages gastronomiques* Paris, La Martinière, 2011.

Catherine Donzel, *Luxury Liners: Life on Board* translated from the French (*Paquebots, la vie à* bord) by Barbara Mellor, Vendome Press, New York, 2006.

Alain A. Grenier, 'Le tourisme de croisière' Les grands équipement touristiques Téoros, 27–2, June 2008, pp. 36–

48, available online at: http://teoros.revues.org/135

Bernhard Huldermann, *Albert Ballin*, Cassel & Company Limited, 1922.

Sonia Kinzler and Doris Tillmann, *Nordlandreise: Die Geschichte einer touristischen Entdeckung*, Mareverlag, 2010.

Arnold Kludas, *Vergnügungsreisen zur See. Eine Geschichte der deutschen Kreuzfahrt*, Band 1: 1889–1939, Convent Verlag, 2001.

John Maxtone-Graham, *The Only Way to Cross*, MacMillan Publishing Company, New York, 1972.

John Maxtone-Graham, *Liners to the Sun*, Sheridan House, 2000.

Daniel Okrent, *Last Call: The Rise and Fall of Prohibition*, Scribner Book Company, 2010.

Peter Quartermaine and Bruce Peter, *Cruise: Identity, Design and Culture*, Rizzoli, 2006.

John T. Reilly, *Greetings from Spitsbergen: Tourists at the Eternal Ice 1827–1914*, Tapir Academic Press, 2009.

John Soennichsen, *Miwoks to Missiles: A History of Angel Island*, Angel Island Association, 2000. [added]

David M. Williams, 'Market Pressures and Innovation: The Orient Steam Navigation Co. and the Development of Pleasure Cruising, 1888–1900', *The Northern Mariner/Le Marin du Nord*, X, n° **4**, October 2000, pp. 1–12.

Picture Credits (incomplete)

Acknowledgements

The author is especially grateful to Arnold Kludas, former director of the library of the German Maritime Museum in Bremerhaven, prolific maritime historian and specialist in the history of German cruises, whose works have been of invaluable help in the identification and dating of numerous photographs from German cruises featured in this volume. He would also like to thank his editor Laure Lamendin, for her unfailing support; Sabine Arqué, for her careful and critical readings of the text; Florence Cailly, for her invariably wise advice; Émilie Boismoreau, for her tireless work on the layout; Marc Walter, for his infallible eye; and Philippe Rollet for his kindly rigour.

In addition, he is indebted to all those who have contributed to the picture research for this project, either by opening up their collections, or by helping to identify specific images; particular thanks go to Aly Bello-Cabreriza, of Carnival Cruise Lines; the collectors Carlos Rey (histarmar.com.ar) and Björn Larsson (timetableimages.com); Malte Witte and his Hamburg–Süd line collection ; Eberhard Stoetzner, historian of the Deutsche Afrika Linien; and finally Karen Majeski, Scott Henderson, and members of the website on Moroccan Judaism, Dafinat.net.

Published in the UK by Scriptum Editions, 2013

An imprint of Co & Bear Productions (UK) Ltd

63 Edith Grove, London, SW10 0LB

www.scriptumeditions.co.uk

Publishers: Beatrice Vincenzini & Francesco Venturi

Translation (from the French): Barbara Mellor

Translation ©Co&Bear Productions (UK) Ltd

First published, in French, by Éditions de La Martinière

– de La Martinière Group, Paris.

Original title: *Croisières; Désirs d'ailleurs*

©Éditions de La Martinière – de La Martinière Group, 2013, for the original work.

Distributed by Thames & Hudson

2 4 6 8 10 9 7 5 3 1

ISBN: 978-1-902686-79-0

Reproduction: Planète Graphique, Rouen

Printed in China